The ABC's of the Prophetic

Prophetic Characteristics

Kimberly Moses

Copyright © 2018 by Kimberly Moses

All rights reserved
Rejoice Essential Publishing
P.O. BOX 512
Effingham, SC 29541
www.republishing.org

All rights reserved. No part of this book may be used or reproduced by any means, graphics, electronic, or mechanical, including photocopying, recording, taping, or by any information storage retrieval system without the written permission of the publisher except in the case of brief quotations embodied in critical articles and reviews.

Unless otherwise indicated, scripture is taken from the King James Version

The ABCs of The Prophetic/Kimberly Moses

ISBN-10: 1-946756-37-7
ISBN-13: 978-1-946756-37-4
Library of Congress Control Number: 2018955009

DEDICATION

I dedicate this book to everyone that supports my ministry and to all my students; past, current, and future. Thank you Tron Moses for supporting me and being my biggest support system.

Endorsements

This book, *The ABC's of the Prophetic* gives direct and clear context of how to be aware of your character as a Christian or a Prophet. I like the way every letter of the Alphabet is used to portray the attributes of the day-to-day life of God's prophets, and the corresponding Bible references and biblical examples of such prophets help drive home the points. This is a book perfect for even children to study because it's the beginning guide to enhancing and activating the believer in you. It will carry you through your journey as a child of God and I'm very blessed to have access to it. ~ Shavonda Tucker

I was given the honor of reading and reviewing the book "*The ABC's of the Prophetic.*" This book was an easy read. The topics were bold, and Scripture went along with every topic. I was more into the topic of bold. I have to learn how to become bolder in my walk with Christ. Another topic I enjoyed reading was forgiveness. I had to learn how to forgive no matter how much it hurts. I also like this topic because it made me realize that God forgave me of my sins, so I have to forgive others of their sins as well. Another topic I read was humility, I don't have that in me yet, but God is still working on me. All in all, this is a really good book to read and to get a better understanding about whatever you want to change in your life. Thanks Prophetess K. ~ April Adams

This book is truly God-sent. The ABC's all represented how prophetic people should live consistently. It explains the heart of God and what He desires for His people. This book gave me information that I did not know and has made me want to pursue my walk with God in a pure way. It lists many scriptures that are great for meditation. God wants our hearts to be pure and this book has helped me with getting there. ~ Kentia Middleton

Contents

FOREWORD..vii

ACKNOWLEDGMENTS..................................xix

INTRODUCTION..1

A:	Anointed............................5
B:	Bold....................................12
C:	Correction.........................18
D:	Directive............................24
E:	Emotional..........................32
F:	Forgiving............................43
G:	Grateful..............................51
H:	Humility..............................61
I:	Intercessor.........................66
J:	Just......................................72

K:	Kingdom-Minded............78
L:	Longsuffering..................83
M:	Meditators......................89
N;	Noble...............................93
O:	Obedient..........................97
P:	Prophesier.....................102
Q:	Quaint............................106
R:	Responsible...................113
S:	Sacrificial......................118
T:	Tranquil.........................123
U:	Unbreakable..................127
V:	Valiant...........................133
W:	Wise...............................137
X:	Xenacious......................142
Y:	Yielded...........................146
Z:	Zealous..........................152

ABOUT THE AUTHOR......................................156

REFERENCES..159

Foreword

"Many writings on the prophetic have focused primarily on the works, function, and grace of the prophet. In contrast, *"The ABC's of the Prophetic"* digs deeper and deals with the idealistic attributes, character, and nature that prophetic people should walk in. Kimberly Moses does an excellent job outlining and detailing individual character strengths that should be exhibited by those with a prophetic anointing upon their life. Most importantly, she has personally walked out the principles taught in this book. Her life is a living testimony of the prophetic power of the Holy Spirit to bring transformation.

Prophets are the most misunderstood people and with the most misunderstood ministry. As you read, you will also receive understanding on the nature, personality, and makeup of those called into a prophetic ministry. Understanding *"The ABC's of the Prophetic"* will strengthen the reader not only to be a person that can prophesy but to live a prophetic life that glorifies God. As you read this book, take time to digest the characteristics of a mature believer in Christ, as depicted with each alphabet. Doing so will challenge you to grow in prophetic grace and Christlike character. I recommend this read to both the novice and advanced prophetic ministers."

Apostle Demontae Edmonds,
Freedom 4 the Nations

ACKNOWLEDGMENTS

This book wouldn't be possible without the inspiration of the Holy Spirit. He gave me the blueprint and I just obeyed as I wrote the manuscript.

2 Timothy 3:16-17 says, "All scripture is given by inspiration of God, and is profitable for doctrine, for reproof, for correction, for instruction in righteousness: That the man of God may be perfect, thoroughly furnished unto all good works."

Introduction

THE CHARACTERISTICS OF THE PROPHET

You are probably reading this book because you may have many questions about the prophetic ministry. Perhaps, you want to gain a greater clarification on true prophets compared to false prophets. You may even have a lot of questions about why you are wired the way you are. This book is designed to answer those questions and beyond. This book is a complement to *Enhancing the Prophetic in You*. In that book, I covered the characteristics of true prophets of God and the fruits of the Spirit. However, inside this book, you will see other major characteristics of prophets and why they do certain things. This book was birthed through many trials that I encountered in my prophetic ministry.

There were times when I questioned who I was in God or dealt with religious spirits on people that tried to test me in God. Each time, God gave me wisdom and His reassurance. I am passionate about prophetic characteristics. Character is everything. Character is truly what you do behind closed doors. Character will determine your longevity in ministry and what type of legacy you will leave after you leave this earth. Many people are anointed but lack character, and so they aren't great ambassadors of Jesus Christ (2 Corinthians 5:20). They do a great job of bringing shame and division in the body of Christ. As the Lord allows me to impart into my spiritual daughters, I teach them about prophetic characteristics. I make sure they aren't shacking up or living with their boyfriends. I make sure they are living a godly life. I teach them to have the presence of the Lord. Many people want the gifts of the Spirit but don't want to be processed.

They want the title of a prophet but are immature. It saddens me as I reflect on the fact that some women that I started off in ministry with are no longer in ministry. They either backslid or cross over into divination and now they are proclaimed psychics. Why did this happen? The answer is that they lacked character. They weren't processed through the school of the Holy Spirit. They weren't yielded to the Holy Spirit. This is why prophetic characteristics are so vital. There is a vast difference between a true prophet of God compared to one who isn't. Don't allow anyone to tell you otherwise. As you read the next chapters, you will see many adjectives to describe prophets. We will go through the English Alphabet, from A to Z. My prayer is that you will allow God to do a transformative work in your life and that you go through the necessary steps in order for God to birth or develop His character in you on a deeper level. Let's pray together now.

Dear Heavenly Father,

I come to you today. I repent if I did anything wrong or grieved Your Holy Spirit. I pray that as I read this book, my heart will be pricked to return fully unto you. I pray that I will wholly surrender my life to you. Lord, I declare and decree that I will yield to You in every area of my life. I lift my hands and declare that they are Your hands. I declare that my eyes are Your eyes. I declare that my mouth is Your mouth. I declare my body will be used for Your Glory. I decree and declare that I will not rush the process of me becoming developed in You. Lord, I want to please you in every way. Lord, bless me to be a great representative of Jesus Christ in the earth. I decree that I will bring you Glory and never shame. Thank you, Father, for transforming me in the image of your Son, Jesus. Amen.

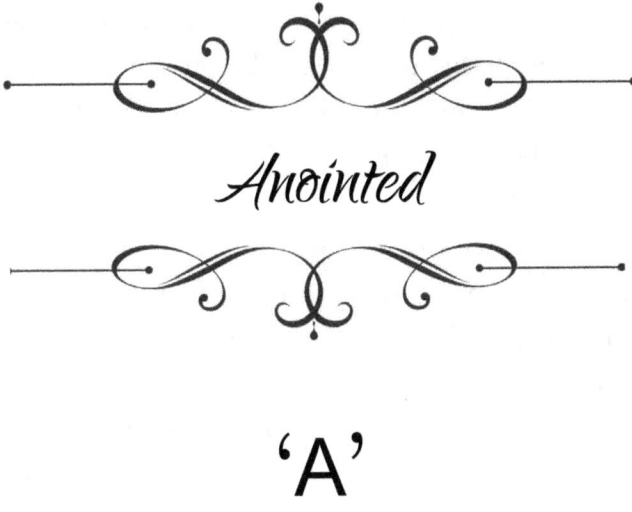

Anointed

'A'

There is a special grace that a prophet has upon their life. Prophets are anointed by God to function and to fulfill their assignment as God's spokespersons. We will explore in this chapter what the anointing is and how God anoints His prophets. The Hebrew word for anointing is Mashach.[1] This word means to rub and to smear. God anoints His prophets with His Spirit and with His presence. It will be very difficult to fulfill the role of a prophet without an anointing from God. Prophets encounter all sorts of warfare and they need the anointing to guard them. Whenever they face resistance, they need the anointing to break through the yokes. When the anointing is operating in the life of a prophet, it makes the task easier to complete.

We can see that various people were anointed and ordained for an assignment. Aaron and his sons were anointed to become priests. They had to wear certain garments when they were anointed and consecrated to become priests (Exodus 29:29). When God anoints a prophet, they are ready for service. This is why a person, who is in the office of a prophet, can prophesy more frequently and more freely than someone that just has the gift of prophecy.

Since they are anointed to prophesy, prophecy just flows out of them. We can see how various people and objects were anointed in Exodus 30:25-29. Oil was placed on the tabernacle, tables, lamp stand, dishes, and any other item that was set apart to be holy unto the LORD. Seeing that prophets are anointed, they have to be set apart. They have to be holy because God anointed them for His use.

David was a prophet and he had to get anointed by God before he could fulfill his purpose. 1 Samuel 16:13 says, "Then Samuel took the horn of oil, and anointed him in the midst of his brethren: and the Spirit of the Lord came upon David from that day forward. So, Samuel rose up, and went to Ramah." Once David got anointed by Samuel the prophet, the Spirit of the Lord came upon him and stayed with him for the rest of his life. It took another prophet to anoint David because they have a special anointing by God to do so.

Prophets, oftentimes, were assigned to appoint leaders and anoint them. Moses was a prophet and anointed his brother Aaron and his sons for the priesthood (Leviticus 8:30). One of the sons of the prophet anointed Jehu to be King (2 Kings 9). Nathan the prophet anointed King Solomon (1 Kings 1:34). In addition, the anointing oil referenced in 1 Samuel 16:13 represents the Holy Spirit, as well as His presence.

It is as if the Holy Spirit is rubbing Himself on His chosen prophets and manifesting His presence through them. Let's look at the ministry of Jesus. He was a prophet (Matthew 21:11). God anointed Jesus with the Holy Spirit and with power. When this occurred, He was given the special ability to function in His ministry at a high capacity. He went around healing the sick and casting out devils. When He became anointed by God, the Lord was with Him even though He was God in the flesh (John 1:1; 14). Acts 10:38 says, "How God anointed Jesus of Nazareth with the Holy Ghost and with power: who went about doing good and healing all that were oppressed of the devil; for God was with him."

One day, I went to a revival service. The woman that preached called me to the altar. She was a prophetess. She asked, "Are you ready to see the full manifestation of God in your life?" I said, "Yes." Immediately, she laid hands on my belly. I fell to the floor and she became drained. Some women around her sat her down and prayed that her strength would be restored. It was as if the anointing on her life imparted into me. When I fell to the floor, the power of God was heavy on me. I was slain in the spirit for a few minutes. The next day, I noticed something different about me. I was intensely hot everywhere. I noticed that it felt as if my skin and bones were on fire. I remember checking the thermostat to see if the heat was on because I never felt that hot before. The heat wasn't on and the heat began to spread to different parts of my body. I can recall the heat spreading to my feet and staying there for hours. Then the heat would spread to my arms and hands.

I prayed, and I realized that when the prophetess laid hands on me, I received impartation. I was baptized with the fire of God (Matthew 3:11). God's fire stayed upon me for three whole days and it began to lift. I cried out to God to never take His fire from upon me and He stayed with me. It has been years since I started to feel the fire of God. I feel His presence every day. God anointed me to become a prophet. There is no denying that He is real. The anointing upon my life makes ministering more effective because it's the Holy Spirit flowing out of me that is touching and blessing His people.

After God anointed me, I started writing books at an accelerated pace. I started getting a plethora of ideas to create products to advance the Kingdom of God. I started prophesying, healing the sick, and casting out devils. Before I was anointed, I was just a broken person who was lonely, depressed, and rejected by others in life.

Ezekiel would always have the presence of God come upon him. He would then have visions and received revelation about things that were on the heart of God (Ezekiel 2:2, 3:24). When Samson's hair grew back, God's Spirit came upon him. Once this occurred, his strength came back, and He was able to kill more Philistines when he died than when he was alive (Judges 16). When the anointing is present, you can do the impossible because God's Spirit will enable you to do things beyond your natural humanly effort. In closing, prophets are anointed by God to complete their assignment and purpose in life.

1. What is the anointing?

___

2. What is the purpose of the anointing?

___

3. How important is the anointing in the life of a prophet?

___

Bold

'B'

Prophets have to be bold in order to operate at the full capacity of the ministry that God is calling them. It's very difficult to declare the word of the Lord being timid. I can recall giving hard words and I could feel the hatred of the people. A spirit of boldness rose up inside of me and I began to declare the word of the Lord even more; it was as the fear of acceptance of people diminished. The Lord will make his prophets bold. Everyone has an inner desire to be liked or to fit in; however, this is not the case of a prophet. Prophets can't worry about being liked because the more they preach the truth of the gospel, the more the people who are religious and carnal will hate them. We can see this in the life of Jesus.

The religious Sadducees and Pharisees hated Him. Here was God in the flesh (John 1). He was doing great works, healing the sick, casting out demons, and blessing the poor (Acts 10:38). Yet, they allowed jealousy and self-righteousness to saturate their hearts and they began to plot evil against Him (Matthew 12:14). Jesus was the ultimate example of a prophet being bold. He wasn't concerned about the laws of the Sabbath when someone was in need of a miracle. When the religious leaders approached him about His disciples being unlawful on the Sabbath, He rebuked them and healed the man with a crippled hand (Matthew 12:9).

What would have happened if Jesus had been timid in such scenarios? He would have allowed these religious leaders to dictate His every move, thus holding Him back from fulfilling what He was sent to do. Also, the man with a crippled hand wouldn't have received his healing. We don't know how long this man had been afflicted before he met with Jesus the healer.

However, the man needed a miracle and only the power of Jesus could've healed him. As we read Matthew 12:1-13, we can even see that it took a high level of boldness to heal this man in front of His enemies. Imagine how tense this atmosphere was. Here were spectators all around, but the power of God showed up. Jesus boldly commanded the man to stretch forth his hand and immediately his hand was restored.

Another example of how Jesus was bold when He rebuked these leaders once again can be found in Matthew 12:22-29, where we can see Jesus cast a demon out of a man. The man who was once bound could now see and talk. The Pharisees said that Jesus was casting out demons by the power of a demon. Jesus, who was bold to act out the word of knowledge that He perceived, corrected them and explained that a devil can't cast out a devil; it is only by the power of God can we cast out devils. We can see in verse 25 that He knew what they were thinking, which is an example of word of knowledge. In verse 28, we can clearly see that the Kingdom of God was demonstrated. Jesus had to be bold in order to demonstrate the Kingdom of God.

Let's look at 2 Kings 6:8-22. We can see how bold Elisha was when he was confronted by the Aramean army. He wasn't afraid. He told his servant not to be afraid and prayed for his sight to see in the realm of the spirit so he could be aware of the Lord's angels assisting them in battle. Elisha faced opposition head on, prayed a bold prayer, and his enemies were blinded. Elisha demonstrated more boldness as he led the Aramean army to the city they were looking for. That's a high level of courageousness. He even prayed for their sight to be restored and he never showed any ounce of fear. Imagine guiding your enemies to a place of safety after they just intended to harm you.

There has to be a high degree of boldness in the life of every prophet. We have a real enemy in the spirit who is constantly scheming against us. We have to be ready and always be prepared to speak as the oracle of the Lord. We can't back down when the enemy throws his attacks. We have to make a stance and stand firm. We have to trust that, if God sends us, then He will back us up and protect us. God wants His prophets to be bold. Reflect on the word of the Lord to Isaiah as you continue along this journey.

Isaiah 41:10 says, "Fear thou not; for I am with thee: be not dismayed; for I am thy God: I will strengthen thee; yea, I will help thee; yea, I will uphold thee with the right hand of my righteousness." God will strengthen you and make you as bold as the Lion of Judah (Proverbs 28:1) as you step out and prophesy.

1. Why must prophets be bold?

_____

_____

_____

_____

_____

2. Describe some incidents in the Bible where prophets had to be bold?

_____

_____

_____

_____

_____

3. In what ways can you become bolder in your Christian and ministry walk?

_____

_____

_____

_____

_____

Correction

'C'

Prophets are called to bring correction. Many people expect prophets just to give jolly words, but that isn't always the case. True prophets will rebuke others as the Spirit of God leads them, whenever and wherever necessary. This is why God told the prophet Ezekiel that he was going to set his face like a flint or the hardest rock. He couldn't get intimidated by what people thought about him. He had to obey God by speaking whatever God told to say (Ezekiel 3:8-9). Interestingly enough, another prophet named Isaiah said he would also set his face like a flint and God would not allow him to be disgraced.

Isaiah 50:7 says, "For the Lord GOD will help me; therefore shall I not be confounded: therefore have I set my face like a flint, and I know that I shall not be ashamed."

Being strong in the Lord is necessary when you have to bring a level of correction or rebuke. God encourages us to preach His word despite what we go through. This involves encouraging others, as well as correcting others to help them stay on the straight and narrow path while being patient with them.

2 Timothy 4:2 says, "Preach the word; be instant in season, out of season; reprove, rebuke, exhort with all longsuffering and doctrine."

Prophets are called to speak the word of the Lord. People won't always like to hear it and even despise them for it. Furthermore, this is the purpose of God's word in our lives, which corrects us when we get off track.

2 Timothy 3:16 says, "All scripture is given by inspiration of God, and is profitable for doctrine, for reproof, for CORRECTION, for instruction in righteousness." (Emphasis added to correction)

Let's look at Amos chapter 4. This prophet had to give words of correction to the people of Samaria. They loved festivals, but their hearts weren't right. They were caught up in tradition. God sent five calamites to get them to repent but, their hearts were so hard. They did what they wanted to do. This prophet had to give a word of correction to show them the extent of God's love, and the need for repentance in the land. Let's look at these five calamites before we give more examples of another prophet bringing correction to God's people.

- Famine (Amos 4:6)
- Drought (Amos 4:7-8)
- Crop disease and locust (Amos 4:9)
- Plague (Amos 4:9)

- Destruction of cities (Amos 4:10)

Amos wasn't liked very much, and he was even told to stop prophesying (Amos 7:13). He didn't allow that to stop him from fulfilling the call and neither can you. Every time I minister, I have to correct people by leading them away from carnality and bringing them under the conviction of the Holy Spirit.

The best illustration to learn rebukes is from Jesus Christ.

- He rebuked the winds and the waves (Matthew 8:26).
- He rebuked fever (Luke 4:38-39).
- He rebuked devils (Luke 4:40-41).
- He rebuked Peter for allowing the enemy to use him (Matthew 16:23).
- He rebuked James and John for operating in the wrong spirit (Luke 9:54-55).
- He rebuked His disciples for their lack of faith (Mark 16:14).

Jesus brought order and correction. It was necessary in order to equip others to do what

He did on a greater scale. People may hate you because of it—but if God is for you, who can be against you (Romans 8:31)? God loves us so much that He raises up prophets to rebuke His people. He doesn't want anyone to perish and neither should you. There is no soul not worth saving.

Revelation 3:19-20 says, "As many as I love, I rebuke and chasten: be zealous therefore, and repent. Behold, I stand at the door, and knock: if any man hear my voice, and open the door, I will come in to him, and will sup with him, and he with me."

1. Why are prophets called to bring correction?

_____
_____
_____
_____
_____

2. What are some benefits that a word of correction can bring to someone's life?

___

___

___

___

___

3. Provide some biblical examples when a prophet was called to bring correction?

___

___

___

___

'D'

Prophets are called to bring direction. Many people that support my ministry will ask me to seek God on their behalf in hope of getting direction in their lives. Most prophecies contain instructions. God wants to bless His people, but He often requires something from us. This can include fasting, praying, sowing, and obedience. For instance, once I was believing God to bless my family because we weren't prospering in certain areas. It required me going on an extended fast. God brought confirmation because a prophet who didn't know anything about this fast told me the exact number of days to fast and told me what I was seeking God for. This was in line with what God had already spoken to me. I obeyed God and He blessed my children to excel academically. He even blessed my husband and me by causing us to prosper in the areas we were trusting Him for help.

Many people don't receive everything God has for them because they didn't follow the instructions God gave them. Perhaps they didn't do anything with the prophecy they received and expected God to do everything. As we step out and obey God, the blessings will follow.

Let's look at some prophets who gave directives in their prophecies. A prophet, one that is in the office of a prophet, will give greater details compared to someone who just has the gift of prophecy. We can see this with the prophet Samuel. He gave very detailed prophecies especially, when Saul lost his father's donkeys. Let's explore 1 Samuel 10. We will then get a greater idea of directive prophecies.

In verse two, Samuel told Saul that he was going to meet two men by an exact location. He even told him what they would say unto him concerning his father's donkey and that his father was worried about him. Let's stop for a minute. Do you see how this prophecy is bringing guidance? Saul knew what to expect.

In verse three, Samuel gave Saul his next steps. This is a directive prophecy at its finest. Samuel told Saul that he would leave the previous location and meet three men on their way to go worship God. He told Saul exactly what the men would be carrying. One man had three goats, the other three loaves of bread, and the third man a bag full of wine. There was no way he could've known this except that it was revealed by God.

In verse four, we see that Samuel instructed Saul to receive the gifts from these men whenever they offered it to him. These instructions helped him to receive his blessing. This is how prophecy works in our lives as well. We know exactly what

God wants to do in our lives and to know our next moves.

In verse five, Samuel told Saul his next moves again. He told him in great detail that he would meet a company of prophets. To clear up any confusion, Samuel told Saul that these prophets would have instruments and they would be prophesying. He even went a step further and told Saul exactly what instruments the prophets would be playing: harps, flutes, tambourines, and lyres. There was no way that Saul could've missed this because the prophecy was so precise.

In verse six, Samuel told Saul that he too would prophesy. He prophesied that Saul would be changed spiritually into another man as the Spirit of the Lord would come upon him.

In verse seven, Samuel prophesied that God would be with Saul after this encounter.

In verse eight, Samuel told Saul to tarry for seven days and he would come unto him. He would be making certain sacrifices unto God.

God gives us directions to prepare us for what is to come. Based on these prophecies, Saul knew exactly God's will for his life. Unfortunately, he didn't stay in His will. Directives in prophecies help us to stay on the right track and not get off course.

Let's look at 1 Kings 17:7-16. God instructed Elijah to go to a new location and meet a widow because He had commanded her to sustain him. Elijah obeyed. When he met the widow, he asked her to give him some water and to make him a small loaf of bread. The widow didn't have much food. In fact, she was preparing to cook her last meal for her family and then die. Yet, she had faith and obeyed the instruction of the prophet. She made him a small loaf of bread first and received God's promises of sustenance. The jar of flour and oil never ran dry. The widow and her family were able to eat many meals. Whenever God gives us instructions, it's an opportunity for Him to bless us.

There was one of the sons of the prophets in 2 Chronicles 20. His name was Jahaziel. The people were seeking God because three different enemies were coming against them. In verses 15-17, he prophesied to everyone not to be afraid. He said that the battle was the Lord's and not theirs. He told them to go to a certain location the next day and stand there. He instructed them not to fight because God would save them. The people followed these instructions and victory was obtained.

In 2 Kings 9, one of the sons of the prophets was instructed by Elisha to go anoint Jehu to be King over Israel. He further prophesied that he was chosen to bring down the house of Ahab and Jezebel. Jehu followed these instructions and the prophecy was fulfilled.

In Luke 24, Jesus appeared to His disciples. He gave them instructions to wait in Jerusalem because the Holy Spirit was coming so they could receive power from heaven (Luke 24:49). His disciples obeyed Him and later received the Holy Ghost with evidence of speaking in tongues (Act 2:1-4).

God is merciful, and He loves us with an everlasting love. God will never lead you astray. Seek

God, develop a strong relationship with Him, and He will use you to give more directives in your prophecies.

John 16:13 says, "Howbeit when he, the Spirit of truth, is come, he will GUIDE you into all truth: for he shall not speak of himself; but whatsoever he shall hear, that shall he speak: and he will shew you things to come." (Emphasis added to guide)

1. What is the significance of a directive prophetic word?

_____
_____
_____
_____
_____

2. Provide a biblical example of a prophet giving a directive word?

_____
_____
_____
_____
_____

3. How can someone increase the amount of details that their prophetic word entails?

_____

_____

_____

_____

_____

Emotional

'E'

Prophets are prone to be emotional. Prophets have emotional highs and emotional lows. Yet, God in His sovereignty provides deliverance to His servants. I wrote a book, Overcoming Emotions with Prayers. This book contains over two hundred prayers based off every emotion that I felt when I went through a wilderness experience. Thankful to God, I obtained victory, deliverance, and learned to not allow my emotions to run my life. Some prophets are moody. They make excuses such as, "The reason I have an attitude is because I am a prophet." Again, there is deliverance for God's prophets. God doesn't want us walking around snapping on people. He wants us to express His love to others.

Let's look at some example of emotionalism. Jonah was a prophet of God. Yet, he took the bait that many of us have by getting in his feelings. When God gave him his assignment to deliver a message to a rebellious nation, he ran (Jonah 1:2-3). Jonah probably felt anxious or uneasiness about his assignment, while he tried to escape God's presence. Prophets must be led by God and not their feelings (Romans 8:14). After Jonah had a near-death experience in the belly of a big fish, he repented. He finally obeyed God. However, after he delivered the message that judgment will hit Nineveh in forty days, the people repented (Jonah 3:3-10).

Jonah became angry when he saw what had just happened (Jonah 4:1). As prophets, we should have the heart of God and want souls to get saved. Jonah was extremely emotional because he even asked God to let him die (Jonah

4:3). Wow. Is it really worth dying over if people respond in a positive way to the message that you preach? Whenever we are in our emotions, it clouds our intellect. Jonah became even angrier when a worm ate the plant that was providing him shade, he wished to die even more (Jonah 4:7-8). God was trying to teach Jonah a lesson. However, Jonah completely missed what God was saying. Allowing our emotions to overtake us will completely shift our focus from the will of God and His plans and purposes for our lives to being so consumed with ourselves. Don't miss what God is trying to show you. Maintain a level head and allow God to do a great work in you.

The next example of a prophet being emotional is Elijah. I can relate because there were times when the Lord used me mightily and the next day, I became discouraged because of a distraction. I had to fight against discouragement with praise and worship. At the end of the day, everything was better than okay. Elijah proved that God was real compared to Baal and Asherah. He killed all the false prophets that were present that day when God answered his prayer by fire (1 Kings 18). This was a huge win for the Kingdom of God. God used Elijah to destroy the enemy's camp. Afterwards, Jezebel heard about what Elijah had done. She threatened him. Elijah fled and didn't even want to live anymore (1 Kings 19).

How could someone that operated in such power allow one threat to discourage them to the point of wanting to die? Just as God was with Jonah, He was also with Elijah. He provided a place of refuge. God will do the same for us and we will dwell with His presence. Don't believe the threats of the enemy. It's time to recognize the power that you walk in.

1 John 4:4 says, "Ye are of God, little children, and have overcome them: because greater is he that is in you, than he that is in the world."

To reiterate, emotions will cause you to forget who you are in God. This is one of the strategies of the enemy. Once we forget the authority that Jesus gave us (Matthew 10:1), then the enemy will step up the attacks.

The next example of a prophet being emotional is Habakkuk. He had a burden like most prophets. However, when he got into his feelings, he acted as if his prayers were hitting the ceiling and that God wouldn't do what He said He was going to do. In other words, he started to complain (Habakkuk 1:1-4).

Habakkuk 1:2 says, "O Lord, how long shall I cry, and thou wilt not hear! Even cry out unto thee of violence, and thou wilt not save!"

Habakkuk 1:4 says, "Therefore the law is slacked, and judgment doth never go forth: for the wicked doth compass about the righteous; therefore wrong judgment proceedeth."

This is a dangerous place to be because we start to doubt God. Doubting has so many negative consequences such as missing out on God's promises (James 1:7). God is very aware of what's going on around you. God will provide deliverance and justice. Whenever we get in our emotions, we tend to think that our prayers aren't effective and will stop praying and believing. We can't give up. Get out of those negative emotions and walk by faith.

The next example of a prophet being emotional is Jeremiah. He is known as the weeping prophet and he is also the author of the Book of Lamentations. He probably wept over the sins of the people and the judgment that was coming (Jeremiah 16:3-4). He probably wept because he was lonely since he wasn't allowed to marry or have children (Jeremiah 16:2). He probably wept because of his overall call as a prophet. He probably wept because it seemed as if no one was hearing him due to the hardness of their hearts. Perhaps, it was the amount of persecution he encountered. Once, he became so emotional that he wanted to quit (Jeremiah 20:9) and even doubted God (Jeremiah 15:18). God provided mercy and did not give up on him. He reassured His servant and provided comfort (Jeremiah 15:19). God is faithful even when we are not. Don't allow your emotions to cause you to lose sight of the faithfulness of God.

2 Timothy 2:13 says, "If we believe not, yet he abideth faithful: he cannot deny himself."

The next example is Ezekiel. He just had an open vision and saw the four living creatures, as well as the Messiah (Ezekiel 1 and 2). However, in chapter 3, he became bitter about his assignment.

Ezekiel 3:14 says, "So the spirit lifted me up, and took me away, and I went in bitterness, in the heat of my spirit; but the hand of the Lord was strong upon me."

God knew exactly how to get all the bitterness and anger out of him. He had His Spirit upon Ezekiel strong. Then Ezekiel was instructed to wait seven days; afterwards, God spoke to him again (Ezekiel 3:15-16). Our assignments are bigger than us. If God didn't feel like we were equipped for the task, then He wouldn't have chosen us. Don't get bitter and refuse to walk in your calling. You will regret allowing emotions to cause you to miss out on destiny.

The next example is Moses. Moses was a mighty prophet with a great task. One day, he became so frustrated that he disobeyed God. This resulted in him not partaking in the blessing of the Promised Land. God told Moses to strike the rock and water flowed from it so everyone in the desert had something to drink (Exodus 17:6).

Exodus 17:6 says, "Behold, I will stand before thee there upon the rock in Horeb; and thou shalt smite the rock, and there shall come water out of it, that the people may drink. And Moses did so in the sight of the elders of Israel."

This miracle wasn't about Moses, but it was for everyone to believe in God, that He was with them; He would provide and take care of them. Moses got in his emotions and missed this very point. God gave Moses specific instructions later on, but since Moses was frustrated, he did what he wanted to do. God told Moses not to strike the rock the second time but to speak to the rock (Numbers 20:8). Since Moses was sick of the people's complaints, he acted out of character calling the people rebels.

Numbers 20:10 says, "And Moses and Aaron gathered the congregation together before the rock, and he said unto them, Hear now, ye rebels; must we fetch you water out of this rock?"

What happened to Moses who spent his whole day ministering unto the people (Exodus 18:13)? He didn't allow the people to frustrate him to the point where he disobeyed God in those days. He had a great love for God's children. Over time, he became weary and just got tired of the people complaining. He struck the rock instead of speaking to it and wasn't allowed to go into the Promised Land (Numbers 20:12). Whenever you feel frustrated, get into a quiet place. Seek the Lord. Allow Him to saturate your mind with His peace. You don't want to miss out on all the great things that God has in store for you because you get burned out.

The last example of a prophet being emotional is Jesus Christ. Jesus is our ultimate example of our faith. He is the reason why we are able to operate in the supernatural and perform great works. He expressed righteous indignation the day He saw people selling things in the temple by flipping over tables.

Matthew 21:12-13 says, "And Jesus went into the temple of God, and cast out all them that sold and bought in the temple, and overthrew the tables of the moneychangers, and the seats of them that sold doves, And said unto them, It is written, My house shall be called the house of prayer; but ye have made it a den of thieves."

This is why there is a righteous indignation that most prophets carry on the inside. The Holy Spirit within us is crying out against injustice and sin. Sometimes, the Lord will cause you to do or say certain things. We might become confrontational and pull-down strongholds. We might engage a level of warfare just to set the captive free. Furthermore, if we get into our emotions, we must make sure it's God-led and not flesh-led.

1. Why are prophets emotional at times?

_____
_____
_____
_____
_____

2. Provide some biblical examples of prophets being emotional?

_____

_____

_____

_____

_____

3. What are the positives and negatives of being emotional in the prophetic ministry?

_____

_____

_____

_____

_____

'F'

Prophets have to practice forgiveness because it's a requirement of our faith in God. God commands us to forgive those who hurt us. We are told to love our enemies and pray for those who despitefully use us (Matthew 5:44). How can we love our enemies? Forgive them. How can we pray for those who despitefully use us? Forgive them. The prophetic word must not be tainted, stemming from a place of pain. Forgiveness ensures that our hearts are pleasing in God's sight and the prophecies coming from us are coming from a pure place. Many prophets have stressed the importance of forgiveness through various prophecies.

Acts 10:43 says, "To him give all the prophets witness, that through his name whosoever believeth in him shall receive remission of sins."

Some prophets prophesied remission of sins through the Messiah (Jeremiah 31:34; Ezekiel 36:25). Forgiveness is a big part of a prophetic lifestyle. All throughout Scripture, we see how various prophets had to forgive. Jesus forgave His crucifers (Luke 23:34). Jesus interceded for the same people who mocked Him; beat Him; spat on Him; cast lots or gambling for His clothes. His forgiveness even included Judas, the one person who betrayed him because He prayed for everyone in Luke 23:34. Jesus demonstrated the love of God and extended the mercy of God. God eventually got glorified as His plans became fulfilled. Jesus also forgave Peter for denying Him three times. He restored him by commissioning him to shepherd His people (John 21:15-17).

The next example is when Jesus forgave the women of adultery (John 8). The crowds were ready to stone her, but Jesus stepped in and gave this woman an opportunity to forsake an adulterous lifestyle. He told her to go and sin no more (John 8:11). Perhaps, this encounter with Jesus was what the woman needed to stop sinning and get right with God. We have to love people and want to see them be restored, set free, and made whole. People need to have an encounter with the Jesus in you. Don't go around stoning people by tearing them apart but preach a simple message of God's forgiveness just like John the Baptist did at Jordan.

Jesus called John the Baptist the greatest prophet (Matthew 11:11). John the Baptist's message was all about forgiveness.

Mark 1:4 says, "John did baptize in the wilderness, and preach the baptism of repentance for the remission of sins."

He did a great work for God. He prepared the way for Jesus as he prepared the people's hearts and minds to receive Him. John told people to repent of their sins and God would forgive them. He would then baptize them. This was a very powerful message that brought hope and redemption. Many people felt unworthy of God's love and condemned of their sins but, once they realized this, all they had to do was repent, and then God would forgive them. The burden of guilt was now being broken. Prophets' messages are sometimes ones filled with hope and redemption just like that of John the Baptist.

Joseph forgave his brothers for selling him into slavery (Genesis 50:20). He was able to see the bigger picture, while looking past the pain (Genesis 43:30). He knew God had a purpose for everything that he endured, and it had to happen in order for him to fulfill his purpose. Joseph could have taken revenge and used his high position as the second-in-command to Pharaoh to execute it. Yet, he knew that God trusted him with responsibility when there was a crisis in the land. If Joseph had allowed unforgiveness to set in, then the vision of his assignment would have been clouded. Don't allow unforgiveness to cloud your vision. Many people are holding onto grudges over one thing someone did to them. We have to recognize the enemy behind the attacks we may face just as Joseph did.

The next example is David and Mephibosheth (2 Samuel 9). Mephibosheth was a descendant of Saul or the son of his best friend, Jonathan. David could have been bitter and destroyed Saul's lineage. However, he forgave Saul for trying to kill him several times (1 Samuel 24-26; 2 Samuel 1) and chose to spare Saul's life when he was presented with an opportunity to kill him. After Saul died, David chose to be kind to the household of Saul. He allowed Mephibosheth to eat from his table, restored his land, and gave him provisions. This was a very admirable thing to do.

Most people will not like someone because of who they are associated with. They make assumptions about a person without even giving them a chance. They assume that the apple doesn't fall too far from the tree. If the grandfather was a devil incarnate, an alcoholic, a murderer, etc., they automatically assume that their descendants are as well. This has happened to me several times. I recall times when people didn't like me because they hated my best friend. If they had given me a chance and got to know me, they would have found out that I was one of the nicest people they have ever met.

Moses forgave his brother and sister for talking about his wife (Numbers 12). Imagine if your family were talking bad about your spouse. You probably would be upset and never talk to them again unless it was necessary. Many families are destroyed because of this. Aaron was a prophet and Miriam was a prophetess. They both heard God, but He was angry with them because they were speaking ill about their leader, Moses. Moses' wife was a non-Israelite and they were upset about it. Since they talked against Moses, the Lord struck Miriam with leprosy. Moses interceded for her and she was sent outside of the city for seven days until she came back. Most people would rejoice if their enemy got sick; however, this is not the will of God. We are to extend mercy and pray for those who are afflicted regardless of the evil they did to us.

God doesn't want us to be angry and bitter. He wants us to radiate His love to others. Don't be a hypocrite. We have to make sure that we are practicing what we are preaching like the prophets we just discussed. You want God to forgive you when you mess up. Extend that same mercy and forgive others (Mark 11:26). It's possible to forgive with God's strength!

1. Why should prophets reinforce forgiveness in their lives?

___

2. What are the setbacks of unforgiveness?

___

3. What are some biblical examples of prophets practicing forgiveness?

_____

_____

_____

_____

_____

Grateful

'G'

Prophets are called to be grateful or be thankful. Things may not be going the way we always expect; however, we can be thankful for the small things or the things we tend to take for granted. We can be thankful to have fellowship with the Holy Spirit, life, health, etc. We are called to be thankful in all things (1 Thessalonians 5:18). This involves thanking God for the closed doors and the disconnections because they could have brought more harm than good. As we are thankful and faithful over what we have, eventually God can trust us with more.

David, Daniel, and Jesus were three prophets that expressed a high level of gratitude. Let's explore David first.

"I will give thanks to you, Lord, with all my heart; I will tell of all your wonderful deeds" (Psalms 9:1).

God wants your whole heart, dear prophet. Will you be able to thank Him in the midst of your storm? Prophets are called to encourage others around them despite what they might be going through. Prophets, sometimes your healing and strength is in ministering to others. Prophets are called to testify of God's goodness and His miracles. If God did it before, then He can do it again.

Psalm 28:7 says, "The Lord is my strength and my shield; my heart trusted in him, and I am helped: therefore my heart greatly rejoiceth; and with my song will I praise him."

Prophets have to be thankful that the Lord is their strength when they feel weak. It's the times when we can lean on God's grace to carry us through that we need to be grateful. We have to be glad that God is constantly shielding us from the attacks of the enemy. Imagine if our spiritual eyes were open to see every fiery dart the enemy throws. It would be very nerve wrecking. God may allow us to see some of the attacks but not all because He doesn't want us to worry. He wants to give us rest.

We can be very thankful that our hearts can trust fully in Him. God will not let us down like people will. He is the one person who we can depend on—He's our rock. We can be thankful because He is our miracle worker and solves our impossibilities. Our heart can rejoice when we think about the Lord and we can sing prophetically unto Him with songs and praises.

Psalm 30:1, 12 says, "I will extol thee, O Lord; for thou hast lifted me up, and hast not made my foes to rejoice over me... To the end that my glory may sing praise to thee, and not be silent. O Lord my God, I will give thanks unto thee for ever."

2 Samuel 22:49-50 says, "And that bringeth me forth from mine enemies: thou also hast lifted me up on high above them that rose up against me: thou hast delivered me from the violent man. Therefore I will give thanks unto thee, O Lord, among the heathen, and I will sing praises unto thy name."

As prophets, we can be thankful that God didn't allow our enemies to have the last laugh. People may have been jealous, didn't understand our assignment, or even tried to sabotage our destinies but God delivered us. When the enemy wanted to kill us, God thwarted his plans; we still have life, so we can declare the works of the Lord (Psalm 118:17). God saves His anointed (Psalm 20:6). No matter what the enemy may have planned against you, the counsel of the Lord stands! The devil can't prevail against what God has ordained.

Prophet, you have been chosen by God. God doesn't allow the enemy to keep us in a state of oppression. We can't afford to get in our emotions. We have plenty of reasons to sing unto God with everything within us. We can be thankful that God gave us victory over the enemy, so we should not hold back our praise. We must thank God in whatever season we are in.

Psalm 107:15 says, "Oh that men would praise the Lord for his goodness, and for his wonderful works to the children of men!"

We can thank God for His love especially after being misunderstood and rejected. It's in those lonely times when we can run to the Father and embrace His love. His arms are always open. We can be thankful for His loyalty. He loves us with an everlasting love (Jeremiah 31:3). He will pursue us relentlessly. He will chastise us when necessary, never giving up on us. We can be thankful that God has chosen to use us as His mouthpieces in the earth.

1 Chronicles 29:12-13 says, "Both riches and honour come of thee, and thou reignest over all; and in thine hand is power and might; and in thine hand it is to make great, and to give strength unto all. Now therefore, our God, we thank thee, and praise thy glorious name."

King David thanked God for wealth and while giving it back to Him. He recognized that God gave his hands the power to create wealth (Deuteronomy 8:18). We can thank God for the provision He has given us, and the one He will give us as the need arises in our daily lives. God always sustains His prophets. He used a widow to sustain Elijah (1 Kings 17:7-16) and sent ravens to feed him (1 Kings 17:6).

We can be thankful that God daily loads us with benefits (Psalm 68:19). We can thank God that He gives power to the faint and increases strength to those with no might (Isaiah 40:29). Prophets can't be down too long about finances because God will cause them to prosper. Be thankful that God is increasing your provision.

Daniel 2:23 says, "I thank thee, and praise thee, O thou God of my fathers, who hast given me wisdom and might, and hast made known unto me now what we desired of thee: for thou hast now made known unto us the king's matter."

Daniel was very thankful that God revealed King Nebuchadnezzar's dream and that everyone's life was spared. The King threatened to put to death all the counselors in his court unless they were able to tell him his dream along with the interpretation. Daniel thanked God for wisdom and power. Prophets have to recognize that it is God who gave them the recognition and the talent. We can thank God for answering us when we inquire of Him. We can be thankful for the level of responsibility He has entrusted us with. We can be thankful that our lives are lives of purpose. Just as God gave Daniel revelation and hidden insight, we can also be thankful that He will entrust us, too, with the secrets of men's heart. We can be thankful that God has developed our gifts and trained us in His righteousness.

Matthew 15:36-37 says, "And he took the seven loaves and the fishes, and gave thanks, and brake them, and gave to his disciples, and the disciples to the multitude. And they did all eat and were filled: and they took up of the broken meat that was left seven baskets full."

Mark 14:23 says, "And he took the cup, and when he had given thanks, he gave it to them: and they all drank of it."

Jesus would always give thanks to the Father before meals. He knew that this was an act of faith by thanking the Father in advance. Since He activated His faith, many miracles were demonstrated, and the people were blessed. He illustrated the perfect example for us to thank God for many things including His atonement. Prophets are thankful that Jesus sacrificed His blood on the cross for their sins. They know that they have been bought with a great price (1 Corinthians 6:20) and their life is not their own.

John 11:41 says, "Then they took away the stone from the place where the dead was laid. And Jesus lifted up his eyes, and said, Father, I thank thee that thou hast heard me."

Jesus thanked God to demonstrate His authority when Lazarus died. He wanted the people to believe that God sent Him. Prophets must thank God for using them. God uses His prophets to do miraculous things, so people can believe that He is real. Prophets, be thankful that you are able to demonstrate the Kingdom of God. As we looked upon David, Daniel, and Jesus, we can see there is much to be thankful for.

1. Why should prophets be grateful?

_____
_____
_____
_____
_____

2. What is the power of remaining grateful or having a level of thankfulness?

_____
_____
_____
_____
_____

3. Provide some biblical examples of prophets being grateful?

_____

_____

_____

_____

_____

'H'

Prophets are called to be humble servants of the Lord. Jesus demonstrated true humility when He took the form of a servant even though He was God in the flesh (Philippians 2:5-8). Since prophets are chosen by God, they are also called to put on compassion, kindness, humility, gentleness, and patience (Colossians 3:12) in their everyday walk.

God expresses multiple times how He has a distaste for the proud but favors the lowly or humble (James 4:6; Psalm 138:6; Proverbs 29:23; Matthew 23:12; 1 Peter 5:5). Humility will keep a prophet's heart right before God. For instance, when people want to idolize a prophet that walks in humility, the prophet will not allow it but make sure that God gets the Glory. The prophet will be certain never to steal the recognition for the miraculous but, will always acknowledge the Lord for the great things that may have occurred.

When a person is proud, they will feel like everything they acquire, be it fame or success, was by their own ability, forgetting God in the process. Being filled with pride is a dangerous place to be because pride comes before destruction (Proverbs 16:18). This is the reason why the Lord raised up various prophets to speak out against it and reminds us to walk in humility.

Micah 6:8 says, "He hath shewed thee, O man, what is good; and what doth the Lord require of thee, but to do justly, and to love mercy, and to walk humbly with thy God?"

Micah prophesied that the Lord showed His people what is good, the wonderful things He had done for them, and what is required of them: to do right to others, be kind, obey God, and be humble.

Genesis 18:27 says, "And Abraham answered and said, Behold now, I have taken upon me to speak unto the Lord, which am but dust and ashes."

Abraham recognized God's sovereignty and was honored to be able to stand in the gap to intercede for a whole city. He approached God with humility and his intercession changed God's plans to destroy Sodom momentarily.

Zephaniah 2:3 says, "Seek the LORD, All you humble of the earth who have carried out His ordinances; Seek righteousness, seek humility. Perhaps you will be hidden in the day of the LORD'S anger."

Prophet Zephaniah had a burden for people to walk uprightly before God since He knew some of the plans of God. Being humble, perhaps, is one way to be hidden in the day of the Lord's anger. True prophets want what God wants and don't want anyone to miss out on the opportunity to get saved, delivered, and to experience the goodness of God.

Numbers 12:3 says, "Now the man Moses was very humble, more than any man who was on the face of the earth."

God worked many miracles through the prophet Moses because of humility. Imagine how the Lord will use you as you remain humble?

2 Samuel 7:18 says, "Then went king David in, and sat before the Lord, and he said, Who am I, O Lord God? and what is my house, that thou hast brought me hitherto?"

King David came from humble beginnings. He was often blown away by the things that God was doing in his life. As you walk in humility, God will do some wonderful things in your life and ministry.

1. Why should prophets be humble?

   _____
   _____
   _____
   _____
   _____

2. What are some consequences of not having humility?

   _____
   _____
   _____
   _____
   _____

3. Provide some biblical examples of prophets being humble?

   _____
   _____
   _____
   _____
   _____

'I'

Prophets were created to be intercessors. They have a special connection to God and access to reach the throne room in Heaven. Most of the prophet's ministry will be spent in prayer and intercession. Throughout Scripture, various people prayed on behalf of others, nations, etc. God reveals hidden information beforehand so His people can intercede against the attacks of the enemy or, for the will of God to be done in the earth.

Prophet Daniel interceded for the forgiveness of the people's sins (Daniel 9:3-5). They were in exile. And Daniel, having read the prophecies of Jeremiah, stood in the gap and prayed so fervently, that archangel Gabriel was sent to him with explanations to the things he was seeking the Lord for. Prophets are called to pray for their land, region, nation, household, etc. because lives are depending on their intercession.

Jesus interceded for His followers in John 17. He prayed for us to be loyal (v. 11), joy filled (v. 13), safe from the evil one (v. 15), ready for service (v. 17), united in the Body (v. 21), perfect unity with His Spirit (v. 23), that His Glory will be revealed to us (v.24), and God's love will be in our hearts (v.26). What Jesus prayed impacted generations and His prayers are still being felt in the land today. Imagine how your intercession can impact the generations to come.

Moses interceded for Israel (Exodus 32:11-13). God trusted him with a nation. God revealed His plans to him before He acted upon them (Amos 3:7). It's our job as prophets to be watchmen in the spirit and to cover our nation in prayer against destruction and the attacks of the enemy. As you continue to be consistent in prayer, the Lord will reveal more of His plans and secrets. The secrets of the Lord belong to the righteous (Deuteronomy 29:29).

Nehemiah interceded on behalf of the Israelites (Nehemiah 1:3-11). Here they were shamed and held captive, and the wall around Jerusalem was destroyed. These things grieved Nehemiah. He cried, prayed, and fasted for several days. He confessed the nation's sins and found favor with God to rebuild the wall. God allows prophets to feel certain things and to be burdened by the things that burden Him, so we can intercede for His will to be done in the earth. Just as Nehemiah prayed for restoration, we can too and also see God restore His promises and plans in our generation.

Elijah prayed to God to show Himself to the people by sending down fire (I Kings 18:36-37). He wanted everyone to know just how real God is. Prophets want the power of God to be demonstrated. They want everyone to get to know God and for His plans in their lives to be fulfilled.

Abraham was able to intercede for the people of Sodom. Since there were a few righteous in the land, the unrighteous people weren't destroyed when God wanted to rid the land of perversion (Genesis 18:20-33).

Even though Isaac was the promised child, Abraham interceded for Ishmael's future (Genesis 17:18). We are called to intercede for our children and their children.

Moses interceded on the people's behalf when there were many crises. He interceded for the water to be good to drink (Exodus 15:25) and for God not to destroy the people when the golden calf was made (Exodus 32:11-14). Let's look at some more powerful examples of prophetic intercession:

- Samuel interceded for Saul all night because the Lord regretted He made him King (1 Samuel 15:11).
- Elijah interceded for a widow's son to be resurrected (1 Kings 17:20).
- Elijah prayed for rain (1 Kings 18:41-43).

- Elisha interceded for a widow's son to be resurrected (2 Kings 4:33).
- David interceded for the people to have deliverance from the plague (1 Chronicles 21:17).
- Joel cried out to God once he saw the effects of the locust invasion (Joel 1:19-20).

1. Why are prophets great intercessors?

_____

_____

_____

_____

_____

2. What are some responsibilities of an intercessor?

_____

_____

_____

_____

_____

3. Provide some Bible examples of prophets being intercessors?

_____

_____

_____

_____

_____

'J'

True prophets of God are just. This means acting or being in conformity with what is morally upright or good; righteous.[2] Prophets are bothered by injustice in the land. Many prophets in the Bible cried out against injustice or the evil in the earth.

Zechariah 7:9-10 says, "Thus speaketh the Lord of hosts, saying, execute true judgment, and shew mercy and compassions every man to his brother: And oppress not the widow, nor the fatherless, the stranger, nor the poor; and let none of you imagine evil against his brother in your heart."

Prophets act as a voice for those people who may not be able to be heard. For instance, widows, orphans, and the poor were considered to be lower class and weren't always treated fairly but taken advantage of by wicked leaders who oppressed them by unfair taxes or taking the possessions they might have had. God raised up prophets to cry out against these evil practices. We are to make sure that our hearts are right before God and we treat others fairly.

In his days, the prophet Jeremiah gave similar prophetic instructions to Israel, just as Zechariah did in his time (Jeremiah 7:5-6; 22:3). God has all His prophets on one accord. We aren't supposed to go around committing violence and murder. We are called to show the love of God.

Ezekiel 22:7 says, "In thee have they set light by father and mother: in the midst of thee have they dealt by oppression with the stranger: in thee have they vexed the fatherless and the widow."

Ezekiel called out the hatred in the people's hearts. Prophets call out sin and lead the people unto repentance. Their ultimate goal is to turn the hearts of the people back unto God so His plan can be fulfilled in their lives. They don't want anyone to die and spend an eternity in hell.

Amos 2:6 says, "Thus saith the Lord; For three transgressions of Israel, and for four, I will not turn away the punishment thereof; because they sold the righteous for silver, and the poor for a pair of shoes."

Amos 5:11 says, "Forasmuch therefore as your treading is upon the poor, and ye take from him burdens of wheat: ye have built houses of hewn stone, but ye shall not dwell in them; ye have planted pleasant vineyards, but ye shall not drink wine of them."

Sometimes prophets have to give words of judgment due to all the injustice in the land. A true prophet of God doesn't enjoy this, but they are obedient to the call of God upon their lives. Amos had to give prophecies of judgment. People were so evil that they sold people for silver and shoes. God wouldn't allow them to enjoy the houses or vineyards gained from oppressing the poor.

Many times, prophets had to give woes. Woes can be divine interjections or used to express grief, regret, or distress.[3] They are grieved when they see the wicked prospering in the land (Psalm 37). They get burdened when they feel as if God isn't doing anything to correct the situation (Habakkuk 1). Prophets will stand up for righteousness and defend the gospel of Jesus Christ. They are bothered when the enemy comes in to pervert the gospel with lies. They hate when God's people are led astray.

Isaiah 10:1 says, "Woe unto them that decree unrighteous decrees, and that write grievousness which they have prescribed."

Isaiah was bothered by the people who make unlawful decrees that made life harder for people.

Micah 2:1-2 says, "Woe to them that devise iniquity, and work evil upon their beds! When the morning is light, they practice it, because it is in the power of their hand. And they covet fields, and take them by violence; and houses, and take them away: so they oppress a man and his house, even a man and his heritage."

Micah was disturbed at the amount of people who were plotting evil and acting out everything they planned. He called out the sin of the people who took the possession of others with violent crimes just because they wanted it.

Nahum 3:1 says, "Woe to the bloody city! It is all full of lies and robbery; the prey departeth not."

Nahum didn't sugarcoat anything. He was straight to the point. He called evil for what it is. Prophetic woes are designed to get the people's attention and it's an opportunity for repentance. Don't allow someone to muzzle your mouth. Continue to cry out against injustice because God created prophets to have burdens for His righteousness to be established in the hearts and minds of the people in the land.

1. Define the term just?

_____
_____
_____
_____
_____

2. Why must prophets be associated with being just?

_____
_____
_____
_____
_____

3. What are the consequences of not being just?

_____
_____
_____
_____
_____

Kingdom-minded

'K'

True prophets of God are Kingdom-minded. They think about ways to advance God's Kingdom and ways to establish it here on earth. They know that they are foreigners here in this land (Leviticus 19:33-34) and they are passing through.

What is referred to as being Kingdom-minded? This is getting to know what the Kingdom is. The Kingdom is synonymous with the Kingdom of heaven. This is knowing who God really is or coming into the knowledge of Him. It's a process that can occur over time as we spend time with the Lord.

Are you willing to take this process? When we are Kingdom-focused, we allow God to rule over our hearts and lives because we are submitted to His authority. We are taking the time and sacrifice to yield to our sovereign God. Did you know that the Kingdom of God is within you? Jesus revealed this when He answered the Pharisee's question about the coming Kingdom. Let's take the steps to make sure that everywhere we go, God goes. Prophets will take God with them everywhere they go: the grocery store, restaurant, school, work, etc. They will take the necessary steps to strengthen the Kingdom within them.

Prophets of old have always spoken a Kingdom message and about the coming of Christ.

Daniel 2:44 says, "And in the days of these kings shall the God of heaven set up a kingdom, which shall never be destroyed: and the kingdom shall not be left to other people, but it shall break in pieces and consume all these kingdoms, and it shall stand for ever."

Daniel 7:27 says, "And the kingdom and dominion, and the greatness of the kingdom under the whole heaven, shall be given to the people of the saints of the most High, whose kingdom is an everlasting kingdom, and all dominions shall serve and obey him."

Daniel said God's Kingdom will never be destroyed and His kingdom would last forever. It doesn't matter what the enemy has planned. It will not prosper but God's agenda will be done on the earth. Let's see how the prophets of old confirmed the prophecies of the Kingdom:

- The prophet Isaiah predicted Christ's birth (Isaiah 9:6-7).
- The prophet Isaiah described the characteristics of His reign on earth (Isaiah 11:1-9).
- Isaiah prophesied that Christ will reign righteously (Isaiah 32:1).
- Ezekiel prophesied the second coming of Christ (Ezekiel 34:24; 37:24).

- Jeremiah also prophesied Christ's reign in the earth (Jeremiah 30:9).
- Amos prophesied the restoration of God's Kingdom (Amos 9:11).
- Micah prophesied that God's Kingdom would reign forever (Micah 4:7).
- Zechariah described the blessings of the Kingdom and the Lord's abiding presence in Jerusalem (Zechariah 8:1-8).
- David said God's Kingdom is established, and He rules over all (Psalm 103:19; 45:6; 145:11-13).

Since true prophets of God are Kingdom-minded, they not only preach about the Kingdom but also demonstrate the power of God on the earth.

1 Corinthians 4:20 says, "For the kingdom of God is not in word, but in power." Prophets will demonstrate God's Kingdom through mighty signs and wonders (Romans 15:19).

Matthew 10:7-8 shows signs that happen when the Kingdom of God has come. When the Kingdom comes, the sick are healed, the lepers are cleansed, the dead are raised, and demons are cast out. When a prophet is Kingdom-minded, they don't have time to be wasting doing carnal things. They want to please the Father.

1. Describe the term "Kingdom-minded"?

_____
_____
_____
_____
_____

2. Why must prophets be Kingdom-minded?

_____
_____
_____
_____
_____

3. What are the dangers associated with having a carnal mind?

_____
_____
_____
_____
_____

Longsuffering

'L'

Prophets have to be patient. It is required. This is why God will show them the future so they can patiently wait for the promise.

James 5:10-11 says, "Take, my brethren, the prophets, who have spoken in the name of the Lord, for an example of suffering affliction, and of patience. Behold, we count them happy which endure. Ye have heard of the patience of Job, and have seen the end of the Lord; that the Lord is very pitiful, and of tender mercy."

If you want a great example of someone being patient, look at the life of a prophet. Yes, they go through a lot of warfare but that comes with the office. You have to be patient, especially if you want to get a word from God. This is what Moses had to do.

Numbers 9:8 says, "And Moses said unto them, Stand still, and I will hear what the Lord will command concerning you." A situation arose where the people who were considered ritually unclean, because they touched an unclean body, wanted to celebrate Passover. They didn't know what to do so they sought out the prophet. God gave them instructions on what they needed to do. As a prophet, many people will come to you for counsel. It's okay to say, "Let me go seek God first and I will get back to you" instead of making up something.

Moses was accustomed to waiting on God and staying in His presence to get answers. He waited seven days for God to speak to him on Mount Sinai

(Exodus 24:16). Most people wouldn't wait that long. He waited 40 years in the wilderness, then he had a supernatural encounter (Acts 7:30). He spent all that time in the wilderness before God gave him his assignment.

We have to learn how to wait on His counsel (Jeremiah 23:18). This will ensure that we have the word of the Lord in our mouths as God's prophets. Let's look at some other examples of how prophets had to wait on God.

- The prophet Abraham waited patiently for his promised child, Isaac (Hebrews 6:15; Romans 4:20; Genesis 21:5).
- Joseph waited for the vision to come to pass (Genesis 37:1-50:26).
- Elisha waited for Elijah's prophecy to come to pass about Ahab's house being destroyed (1 Kings 21:21; 2 Kings 9:7).
- Daniel had to wait 21 days for an answer after he fasted (Daniel 10:12-13).
- Habakkuk had to wait for God to give him a vision concerning the solution to the injustice in the land (Habakkuk 2).

- Ezekiel had to wait and be a watchman on the wall (Ezekiel 3:17; 33).
- David had to wait to be king even though he was already anointed (1 Samuel 16; 2 Samuel 5:4).
- Anna had to wait to see baby "Messiah" Jesus (Luke 2:36-38).
- Jesus waited 30 years to officially begin His ministry (Luke 3:23).

The prophet Hosea told people to wait on God. This is a common message that prophets preach. Hosea 12:6 says, "Therefore turn thou to thy God: keep mercy and judgment and wait on thy God continually." The prophet Isaiah proclaimed that he would wait patiently on the Lord despite what the other nations were doing (Isaiah 8:17). Isaiah tells people how patient the Lord was with them as He waited for them to repent and come back to serve Him (Isaiah 30:18).

The prophet Jeremiah knew that, as he waited on the Lord, he would receive hope (Lamentations 3:24-26). The prophet Micah knew that, as he waited on God, he would receive help (Micah 7:7). David knew that he would get strength by waiting on the Lord (Psalm 27:14). He also knew that he would patiently wait for the Lord to receive honor, blessing, inheritances, or great things. He didn't want to get distracted about the wicked prospering because he knew that their future wasn't bright (Psalm 37:7, 34). He depended on God so he didn't mind waiting on Him (Psalm 123:2). Prophets can't fall apart when it seems like the wicked are being blessed and they aren't. They can't lose all hope and lose confidence in God when they go through a challenge. As you wait on God, prophet, He will come through and deliver you.

1. Define the term longsuffering?

_____

_____

_____

_____

_____

2. Why must prophets be longsuffering?

3. What are the dangers of moving ahead of God?

'M'

Daniel knew the word of God. He familiarized himself with the prophecies of Jeremiah (Daniel 9:2). When was the last time you meditated on Scripture? Prophets have to meditate on the word of God to be effective in ministry. They are not their own and they have to have a clear head in order to hear God. A true prophet will want to please God and it begins with their heart being pure and having the right thoughts. This means that there is no place for doubt or fear to be planted in their minds. David was a powerful prophet that had the heart of God. Psalm 19:14 says, "Let the words of my mouth, and the meditation of my heart, be acceptable in thy sight, O Lord, my strength, and my redeemer."

Prophets get joy when they meditate on God and think about His wondrous ways. Psalm 104:34 says, "My meditation of him shall be sweet: I will be glad in the Lord." Prophets meditate on God late in the night to encourage themselves because they know that He is their help. Psalm 63:6 says, "When I remember thee upon my bed, and meditate on thee in the night watches."

Prophets have to meditate on the Word when they study it. They enjoy studying the word of God because it refreshes them. Psalm 111:2 says, "The works of the Lord are great, sought out of all them that have pleasure therein." They know that meditation is the key to getting the word of God embedded in their hearts. Prophets know God's ways; not just His acts. Psalm 119:15-16 says, "I will meditate in thy precepts, and have respect unto thy ways. I will delight myself in thy statutes: I will not forget thy word."

In tough times, prophets remember what God did for them in the past. Psalm 143:5 says, "I remember the days of old; I meditate on all thy works; I muse on the work of thy hands." They know if God did it before, then He can do it again. As they take the time to meditate, their faith is increased, and they are able to encourage others around them. Psalm 145:5 says, "I will speak (think) of the glorious honour of thy majesty, and of thy wondrous works."

As you take the time out to meditate on a daily basis, your prophetic gift will increase. You will be able to prophesy the word of God on a higher level. Out of your belly will flow rivers of living water. Whatever scriptures that you took the time to meditate on, the Holy Spirit will bring it back unto your remembrance.

1. What is meditation?

_____
_____
_____
_____
_____

2. How does meditation apply to the life of a prophet?

3. What are the adverse effects of not meditating on the word of God?

Noble

'N'

True prophets of God have noble character. Noble can be defined as possessing outstanding qualities.[4] Outstanding qualities are a great attribute to have in today's society. There is so much wickedness in the land; nobleness seems rare. However, there are still some prophets of today with noble character. To be noble is to have integrity, walk blamelessly, and have God's heart. When you have noble character, you will do the right thing in tough situations.

David was considered noble, this is why God said he was a man after his heart (1 Samuel 13:14). When you are noble, you will refuse to defile your body. You will choose to remain pure. For instance, Daniel refused to eat the King's food because it would have defiled his body. Daniel 1:8 says, "But Daniel purposed in his heart that he would not defile himself with the portion of the king's meat, nor with the wine which he drank: therefore he requested of the prince of the eunuchs that he might not defile himself." When you are noble, you do not follow the crowd but stand true to godly principles.

Noble character blesses us to make wise choices that are pleasing to God. Proverbs 11:3 says, "The integrity of the upright shall guide them: but the perverseness of transgressors shall destroy them." When you are noble, you will trust God no matter what and stay on the right path despite adversity. Proverbs 10:9 says, "He that walketh uprightly walketh surely: but he that perverteth his ways shall be known." You will walk securely.

When you are noble, you will pass every test that arises (Proverbs 17:3). These tests consist of issues of the heart which can be pride, lust, greed, truth, love, etc. A noble prophet will allow the Holy Spirit to take them through the necessary sanctification process. They will also be strengthened when they go through various trials because more character is being developed in them. Their minds are full of the word of God (Philippians 4:8). These prophets will practice righteousness (2 Peter 1:5-6).

Noble prophets are a great example to follow (Isaiah 32:8) and they encourage others to follow them as they follow Christ. They are considered a great role model and many people are motivated by their lifestyle to seek God more and to walk uprightly before Him (Titus 2:7-8).

God is pleased when you have noble attributes. 1 Chronicles 29:17 says, "I know also, my God, that thou triest the heart, and hast pleasure in uprightness. As for me, in the uprightness of mine heart I have willingly offered all these things: and now have I seen with joy thy people, which are present here, to offer willingly unto thee." Continue to practice righteousness. Always choose God over money. Close the door to sin in your life. Don't allow yourself to be influenced to do sinful things associated with ungodly people. Continue to fight the good fight of faith.

1. Define the word noble?

_____
_____
_____
_____
_____

2. What are some blessings of being noble?

_____
_____
_____
_____
_____

3. How important is it to be noble in life?

_____
_____
_____
_____
_____

Obedient

'O'

Prophets have to be obedient to God. This is one of the biggest attributes of the prophetic office. Prophets don't belong to themselves but to God. Prophets have to go through various trials to learn obedience. Jesus learned obedience through the things He suffered. Hebrews 5:8 says, "Though he were a Son, yet learned he obedience by the things which he suffered." Prophets have to speak what God tells them to speak.

Deuteronomy 18:18-19 says, "I will raise them up a Prophet from among their brethren, like unto thee, and will put my words in his mouth; and he shall speak unto them all that I shall command him. And it shall come to pass, that whosoever will not hearken unto my words which he shall speak in my name, I will require it of him."

Prophets have to do things that may be out of their comfort zone. God told prophet Hosea to buy his wife back after she committed adultery (Hosea 3). He obeyed God. Most people wouldn't want their adulterous spouse back. They would be very reluctant to do what Hosea did. Prophets have to follow God even when it's difficult or when they don't understand it. Everything that God told Hosea had a purpose. His whole marriage to Gomer was symbolic of God's relationship with Israel.

God used Ezekiel as a sign when his wife died. He had to mourn silently. The same thing Ezekiel had to go through, the people would also face the same fate (Ezekiel 24:15-24). Imagine if your whole life was a sign and God used you as an example. However, God is merciful. He warned Ezekiel what was going to happen suddenly, which was the passing of his wife. God warns prophets of what is to come and it's up to us to obey Him.

Many people want to follow their hearts and do fleshly things. Would you be willing to follow after God if you had to deny yourself and live a sacrificial lifestyle? God told Jeremiah not to marry or have children. He obeyed (Jeremiah 16:2). God isn't cruel, but He knew what was best for Jeremiah and for us. He knew Jeremiah couldn't have a family to fulfill the purpose on his life. When God tells you something, obey! You don't want to miss out on purpose.

Abraham paid the ultimate sacrifice by leaving everything he was familiar with just to follow God (Genesis 12). Most people would want to hold on to their past and would have a hard time with this. Prophets want God more than anything else or anyone else. They are willing to pay the price and obey God's command. They know that there are consequences for disobedience (Deuteronomy 28:15-64). Prophets want others to obey God

(Jeremiah 7:25-26) so they can experience His best for their lives.

1 Kings 2:3 says, "And keep the charge of the Lord thy God, to walk in his ways, to keep his statutes, and his commandments, and his judgments, and his testimonies, as it is written in the law of Moses, that thou mayest prosper in all that thou doest, and whithersoever thou turnest thyself." David said these words on his deathbed.

Malachi 2:2 says, "If ye will not hear, and if ye will not lay it to heart, to give glory unto my name, saith the Lord of hosts, I will even send a curse upon you, and I will curse your blessings: yea, I have cursed them already, because ye do not lay it to heart." The prophet Malachi prophesied these very words. All of God's prophets will tell you to obey His commands. Whenever you obey God, the blessings follow.

1. Why must prophets be obedient to God?

2. What are the consequences of disobedience?

3. Provide some biblical examples of prophets being obedient to God?

Prophesier

'P'

Prophets speak the thoughts of God. Everything they prophesy is confirmed by the word of God or God confirms what they speak. There were many prophecies about Jesus' coming by various prophets in the Bible. Zechariah, Isaiah, and Malachi were some prophets that prophesied the coming of the Messiah.

- Isaiah prophesied the virgin birth (Isaiah 7:14).

- Hosea prophesied that the Messiah would end up in Egypt (Hosea 11:1).
- Micah prophesied that the Messiah would be born in Bethlehem (Micah 5:2).
- David prophesied that the Messiah will be humbled to save mankind (Psalm 8:5-6).
- David prophesied the sacrifice that the Messiah would make (Psalm 40:6–8).
- Isaiah prophesied that the Messiah's ministry would begin in Galilee (Isaiah 9:1–2).
- Isaiah prophesied that the Messiah would have a miracle ministry (Isaiah 35:5–6).
- Isaiah prophesied the "Forerunner" or John the Baptist would come before the Messiah (Isaiah 40:3–4).
- Isaiah prophesied that the Messiah would be a redeemer of the Gentiles (Isaiah 42:1–4).
- Isaiah prophesied that the Messiah would be despised and rejected (Isaiah 53:3).
- Isaiah prophesied that the Messiah would set the captives free (Isaiah 61:1).
- Daniel prophesied that the Messiah would have an everlasting throne (Daniel 7:13–14).

- Daniel prophesied that the Messiah would bring an end to sin (Daniel 9:24).
- Zechariah prophesied that the Messiah would ride on a donkey (Zechariah 9:9).
- Zechariah prophesied that the Messiah would be betrayed for 30 pieces of silver (Zechariah 11:12–13).
- Moses prophesied that the Messiah's blood would be shed for atonement (Leviticus 17:11).
- Isaiah prophesied that the Messiah would conquer death (Isaiah 25:7–8).
- Isaiah prophesied that the Messiah would be mocked and abused (Isaiah 50:3–6).
- Isaiah prophesied that the Messiah would pour out His Spirit (Isaiah 44:3).
- Jeremiah prophesied that the Messiah would usher in a new covenant (Jeremiah 31:31).
- Joel prophesied that God would pour out His Spirit upon all flesh (Joel 2:28).

As you see above, there were many prophecies about the Messiah that were fulfilled. Just as Moses was a voice that gave the people the living oracles or word of God (Acts 7:38), so will your voice be. You will be God's oracle as you proclaim His word. You were born to prophesy!

1. What are some things that the prophets of old prophesied?

   _____
   _____
   _____
   _____
   _____

2. What are the benefits of a prophetic word?

   _____
   _____
   _____
   _____
   _____

3. Define the term oracle?

   _____
   _____
   _____
   _____
   _____

'Q'

Prophets are very quaint. This means that they are considered odd, unusual, or different in appearance or character.[5] Prophets don't fit the average mold. They can't listen to everything such as the music the world listens to. They can't watch everything such as the movies the world watches. They are considered strange because they are different. They have been set apart for God's use and staying consecrated is their goal.

Deuteronomy 14:2 says, "For thou art an holy people unto the Lord thy God, and the Lord hath chosen thee to be a peculiar people unto himself, above all the nations that are upon the earth." Prophets are very peculiar people because they aren't conformed to the ways of the world.

Every day, prophets must renew their minds so they won't be conformed to the ways of the world.

Romans 12:2 says, "And be not conformed to this world: but be ye transformed by the renewing of your mind, that ye may prove what is that good, and acceptable, and perfect, will of God."

Prophets are considered quaint because they stick to the "old-time religion" of a consecrated lifestyle—a life sold out to God and in opposition to worldliness. Prophets don't want go to parties or do things that lukewarm or cold believers would do. They are not going to be carried away by the lifestyle of our modern-day, ungodly society.

1 Peter 2:9 says, "But ye are a chosen generation, a royal priesthood, an holy nation, a peculiar people; that ye should shew forth the praises of him who hath called you out of darkness into his marvellous light."

Prophets are God's chosen vessels and have His hand upon their lives.

Deuteronomy 7:6 says, "For thou art an holy people unto the Lord thy God: the Lord thy God hath chosen thee to be a special people unto himself, above all people that are upon the face of the earth."

They will never fit in with the crowd because God has set them apart. Exodus 19:5 says, "Now therefore, if ye will obey my voice indeed, and keep my covenant, then ye shall be a peculiar treasure unto me above all people: for all the earth is mine." Prophets are considered quaint because they are extremely obedient to God. The average person struggles with obeying the voice of the Lord.

Deuteronomy 26:18 says, "And the Lord hath avouched thee this day to be his peculiar people, as he hath promised thee, and that thou shouldest keep all his commandments."

Let's look at John the Baptist. He was very peculiar. He wore clothing out of camel's hair and ate locust and honey (Matthew 3:3-4). He looked untamed and didn't look like the priests or religious leaders; yet, God used him mightily. He spent his whole ministry in the wilderness outside of the traditional religious setting. Whenever prophets do something outside of the traditional setting, it's considered odd or out of the norm. Prophets are led by God's Spirit just as John the Baptist was.

Elijah was different from the other prophets in his day because most of them served false gods and he never bowed down to Baal or Asherah. Instead, he killed 450 prophets of Baal and 400 prophets of Asherah (1 Kings 18). King Ahab called him a troublemaker (1 Kings 18:17). Elijah was very quaint because he didn't yield to the wicked ways of the land, nor did he try to fit in with the false prophets. It was God's will for him not to fit in but be different. Whenever you walk in God's will, you become a threat to the enemy's kingdom.

Ezekiel's prophetic behavior was concerned quaint too. God used him to behave oddly to get His message across to the people. He was told to cut his hair which was out of the norm. He had to separate his hair in one thirds and follow the instructions of the Lord (Ezekiel 5). He had to cook his food on animal dung (Ezekiel 4). He acted like he was being taken into captivity. His ways seemed odd to the crowd. However, God was with him and blessed him because of his obedience.

Abraham spent a lot of time with God (Genesis 15). Most people will think that's weird or that he was extremely religious. He wasn't religious but had a hunger for God. Don't allow people to diminish your hunger for the things of God because you want more of His presence. The world can't comprehend the things of the Spirit because it is foolish to them. What's normal to the world is to watch television all day, but what's normal to a prophet is to spend hours in prayer dwelling in God's presence.

Moses spent a lot of alone time on the mountain. Most people aren't willing to make that sacrifice. Since he constantly sought after God, he was blessed to write the Ten Commandments. Making sacrifices for the Kingdom of God is considered odd to the world, but it's not for God's prophets. They know that God honors sacrifices. Continue to be who God called you to be and never change to be liked by the crowd.

1. Define the term quaint?

_____
_____
_____
_____
_____

2. How are prophets unusual at times?

_____
_____
_____
_____
_____

3. What ways can prophets stay encouraged in their prophetic ministry when they don't fit in with the crowd?

_____
_____
_____
_____
_____

'R'

Being a prophet is a huge responsibility because prophets provide guidance and so it's important that they don't lead anyone astray. It's not about the fame or the public success. It's not about the riches or the financial gain. It's not about being liked or preaching on the biggest stages. It's about making sure that you are in the assignment God gave you. It's about seeking the face of God on a continual basis and yielding your life to Him. This office isn't for someone with the wrong motives, but it's for those who God calls.

The majority of a prophet's ministry is spent in prayer. Most prophets are up during the late hours of the night or the early hours of the morning engaged in warfare. God is showing them things to come or things to pray against. God is exposing the enemy's plans. God is giving them a burden to pray for and to intercede for various things He places on their hearts. Prophets are called to be watchmen on the wall (Ezekiel 33). They are spiritual gatekeepers. They have to wait and watch in prayer. They have to wait for what God will show them (Habakkuk 2).

If the prophet is asleep on their posts, then that blood will be on their hands. For instance, if a prophet is called to cover a certain congregation in prayer and certain spirits creep in due to the lack of prayer there, then that prophet will be responsible. God told that prophet to pray for that congregation but they didn't keep watch. They were asleep when they should have been praying. They stopped praying because they got distracted. Contrarily, if that prophet had been on his post, then he would have seen the spirit creeping in.

Prophets are a voice for people who may not be heard due to social status and the lack of access to leaders or people in high positions. These prophets are voices to the poor, widowed, outcasts of society, and the lost. Prophets cry out against injustice. They feel righteous indignation for things that grieve God's heart. Prophets will expose the wickedness in the earth and warn people to repent. Isaiah 58:1 says, "Cry aloud, spare not, lift up thy voice like a trumpet, and shew my people their transgression, and the house of Jacob their sins."

Prophets will anoint leaders and help guide the leader to choose the right person for the job. They are called to equip others to do the work of ministry effectively (Ephesians 4). Prophets want others to be prophets.

Numbers 11:29 says, "And Moses said unto him, Enviest thou for my sake? would God that all the LORD'S people were prophets, and that the LORD would put his spirit upon them!"

Prophets have to carry the secrets of the Lord because they are His chosen messengers. They will be held accountable for that word that God gave them. Did they pray over that word? Did they release that word in God's timing? Did they follow God's instructions when releasing the word? Can God trust them with the word?

Prophets proclaim the truth of God's word. If they preach anything outside of God's word, then that prophet will be judged. Their main assignment is to turn people's hearts back unto God.

2 Timothy 3:16-17 says, "All scripture is given by inspiration of God, and is profitable for doctrine, for reproof, for correction, for instruction in righteousness: That the man of God may be perfect, thoroughly furnished unto all good works."

1. Why must a prophet be responsible?

   _____

   _____

   _____

   _____

   _____

2. What are some functions of a prophet?

   _____

   _____

   _____

   _____

   _____

3. What are some dangers of being irresponsible?

   _____

   _____

   _____

   _____

   _____

Sacrificial

'S'

Prophets have to live sacrificial lifestyles. Are you willing to make the sacrifices required as a prophet? It's a great price to pay but the rewards are worth it.

2 Corinthians 6:17 says, "Wherefore come out from among them, and be ye separate, saith the Lord, and touch not the unclean thing; and I will receive you."

They have to deny their flesh and carnal things.

Galatians 5:24 says, "And they that are Christ's have crucified the flesh with the affections and lusts."

If they feel sensual, they must deny themselves of fornication because they want to please God. If they get tempted with certain sinful pleasures, they must turn it down because they belong to God. Since prophets have the hand of the Lord upon them, they have to live a sacrificial life.

Jeremiah 15:17 says, "I sat not in the assembly of the mockers, nor rejoiced; I sat alone because of thy hand: for thou hast filled me with indignation."

Prophets will sacrifice their desires for God's. They will put their agenda on the backburner and pick up God's. They will give up things for God. They will sacrifice careers, family, finances, and more. Abraham had to separate from Lot (Genesis 13). Prophets are willing to pay the price for the anointing on their lives. The disciples in the Bible left their businesses to follow after Jesus (Matthew 4:18-22). Prophets will sacrifice certain things in order to fulfill the call of God on their lives. Jeremiah was commanded not to marry or have children (Jeremiah 16:2).

Prophets must serve without expecting anything in return. Money is not their motive for serving. They serve because they are called by God. They truly want people to be blessed so they don't mind giving their time. Prophets may sometimes have to sacrifice time away from certain gatherings or family to fulfill their assignment.

Psalm 102:7 says, "I watch, and am as a sparrow alone upon the house top."

They will sacrifice by abstaining from food to seek God.

Jeremiah 16:8 says, "Thou shalt not also go into the house of feasting, to sit with them to eat and to drink."

The ABCs Of The Prophetic

Prophets need quiet time to be alone with God (Mark 1:35-37). They have to make sure they are in God's counsel because it's their life line.

John 15:5 says, "I am the vine, ye are the branches: He that abideth in me, and I in him, the same bringeth forth much fruit: for without me ye can do nothing."

When you live a sacrificial lifestyle, God will bless you.

Psalm 1:1 says, "Blessed is the man that walketh not in the counsel of the ungodly, nor standeth in the way of sinners, nor sitteth in the seat of the scornful."

1. Why do prophets have to live a sacrificial lifestyle?

_____
_____
_____
_____
_____

2. What are some biblical examples of prophets making sacrifices?

3. What are some dangers of not living a sacrificial lifestyle as a prophet?

'T'

Prophets that are mature have a tranquil mindset. The term tranquil can be defined as free from agitation of mind or spirit; self-assurance; free from disturbance or turmoil.[6]

Philippians 4:6-7 says, "Be careful for nothing; but in every thing by prayer and supplication with thanksgiving let your requests be made known unto God. And the peace of God, which passeth all understanding, shall keep your hearts and minds through Christ Jesus."

Prophets have learned over time to not stress themselves over things out of their control. They've learned how to rest in God. They trust God with everything within them. When a prophet is in the right frame of mind, they are able to advance God's Kingdom. They are able to stay the course of their assignments regardless of what they may be facing.

Prophets keep their minds on God because Christ is their focus. Christ is their center for everything they do. Since they are focusing on Jesus, they have peace despite of what may be going on around them.

Isaiah 26:3 says, "Thou wilt keep him in perfect peace, whose mind is stayed on thee: because he trusteth in thee."

Prophets have the mind of Christ therefore they experience a level of freedom and peace.

John 14:27 says, "Peace I leave with you, my peace I give unto you: not as the world giveth, give I unto you. Let not your heart be troubled, neither let it be afraid."

Prophets recognize the attacks of the enemy. They know that they have to cast down those high imaginations and bring their thoughts into subjection of God's word.

2 Corinthians 10:5 says, "Casting down imaginations, and every high thing that exalteth itself against the knowledge of God and bringing into captivity every thought to the obedience of Christ."

Prophets refuse to allow demonic seeds or wicked thoughts to be planted. They refused to be distracted because they need to be in a steady state to be able to hear the voice of God.

1. Define the term tranquil.

2. Why is having tranquility important?

3. How can someone overcome the attacks of the enemy or attacks in their mind?

'U'

Prophets have to stand strong in persecution. This makes them unbreakable.

2 Corinthians 4:8-9 says, "We are troubled on every side, yet not distressed; we are perplexed, but not in despair; Persecuted, but not forsaken; cast down, but not destroyed."

Trouble will not stop what God wants to do through His prophets. Prophets have to continue to deliver the prophetic word even when they experience persecution.

Matthew 5:12 says, "Rejoice, and be exceeding glad: for great is your reward in heaven: for so persecuted they the prophets which were before you."

Prophets know that persecution comes with the calling.

2 Timothy 3:12 says, "Yea, and all that will live godly in Christ Jesus shall suffer persecution."

They know that they have to go through suffering because Jesus went through it. They know that they must share in the suffering of Jesus.

1 Peter 4:13 says, "But rejoice, inasmuch as ye are partakers of Christ's sufferings; that, when his glory shall be revealed, ye may be glad also with exceeding joy."

Prophets will be hated for the message they preach.

John 15:18 says, "If the world hate you, ye know that it hated me before it hated you."

Some of their message will not be received. They will have to shake off the dust and keep it moving to their next assignment.

Matthew 10:14 says, "And whosoever shall not receive you, nor hear your words, when ye depart out of that house or city, shake off the dust of your feet."

Prophets don't have time to get discouraged about the call. Yes, it may hurt at times but as they stay in God's presence, then they will receive healing in their emotions.

Psalm 62:6 says, "He only is my rock and my salvation: he is my defense; I shall not be moved."

Prophets know that God is their defense. They know that as long as they are in His will, then they will be safe. Prophets know that they have to set their face like a flint as they cry out loud and spare not.

Psalm 16:8 says, "I have set the Lord always before me: because he is at my right hand, I shall not be moved."

Prophets keep their focus on God and they receive strength to fulfill the assignment.

Psalm 18:32 says, "It is God that girdeth me with strength, and maketh my way perfect."

Proverbs 10:30 says, "The righteous shall never be removed: but the wicked shall not inhabit the earth."

God will establish His prophets and remove their enemies so they can complete their assignment.

Proverbs 12:7 says, "The wicked are overthrown, and are not: but the house of the righteous shall stand."

Prophets must keep their hearts right and pray for their enemies.

Matthew 5:44 says, "But I say unto you, Love your enemies, bless them that curse you, do good to them that hate you, and pray for them which despitefully use you, and persecute you."

Prophets are blessed regardless of the trials they face (1 Peter 4:12-14; Matthew 5:10; 1 Peter 3:14; Luke 6:22). Prophets, your work is not in vain. Remember you are unbreakable.

1. Why must prophets be unbreakable?

_____
_____
_____
_____
_____

2. What are some examples of the warfare prophets encounter?

_____

_____

_____

_____

_____

3. What are some strategies to stand firm in the faith?

_____

_____

_____

_____

_____

Valiant

'V'

Prophets have to be valiant. This can be defined as possessing or acting with bravery or boldness: courageous valiant soldiers; marked by, exhibiting, or carried out with courage or determination.[7] The word of God expresses "being valiant" on multiple occasions. Let's explore some of these occasions. In Numbers 24:18, Israel would do valiantly when their enemies tried to rise up against them. No matter how bad Balak wanted Balaam to curse them, he couldn't. As prophets, you have to be brave regardless of the attacks of the enemy.

In 1 Chronicles 19:13, David had to be valiant when his men were humiliated and took advantage of. As a result of his bravery, he was victorious. Will you allow the enemy to harass, embarrass, and destroy the ones that you care about? This is why prophets have to be valiant because they will stand up for injustice and war accordingly in prayer or confrontation by the unction of the Holy Spirit.

Prophets must know that God is fighting their battles and they must not lose focus.

Psalm 60:12 says, "Through God we shall do valiantly: for he it is that shall tread down our enemies." With the prophetic anointing, there will come threats but the prophets must know that God will protect them (Psalm 108:13). Prophets know that with God, they will do great exploits. They will not be stopped from completing their tasks (Daniel 11:32).

Prophets must not lose their joy or peace while they are doing their assignment. God is backing them up. When they feel discouraged, they have to remember that God will do powerful things. God will do the miraculous through His prophets.

Psalm 118:15-16 says, "The voice of rejoicing and salvation is in the tabernacles of the righteous: the right hand of the Lord doeth valiantly. The right hand of the Lord is exalted: the right hand of the Lord doeth valiantly."

Remember to stay bold and do not let adversity stop you. Through God, prophet, you will do valiantly.

1. Define the term valiant.

_____
_____
_____
_____
_____

2. How does being valiant apply to the life of a prophet?

_____

_____

_____

_____

_____

3. Why must prophets trust God to fight their battles?

_____

_____

_____

_____

_____

'W'

Wise

God gives wisdoms to His prophets. For instance, prophets Heman [(Ethan) 1 Kings 4:31] and Daniel (Daniel 1:17) were considered very wise. Prophets will know when to release a word or when to be silent when they seek God for His counsel. Prophets will even gain wisdom for ministry, counseling, finances, relationships, and other areas. Godly wisdom is different from worldly wisdom.

James 3:17-18 says, "But the wisdom that is from above is first pure, then peaceable, gentle, and easy to be intreated, full of mercy and good fruits, without partiality, and without hypocrisy. And the fruit of righteousness is sown in peace of them that make peace."

God's wisdom is able to help those who may be troubled or in need of direction. Prophets have a special ability to walk in this wisdom.

The prophet Isaiah prophesied that Jesus would have the spirit of wisdom poured out upon Him.

Isaiah 11:2 says, "And the spirit of the LORD shall rest upon him, the spirit of wisdom and understanding, the spirit of counsel and might, the spirit of knowledge and of the fear of the LORD."

Jesus was able to increase in wisdom and we can as well.

Luke 2:52 says, "And Jesus increased in wisdom and stature, and in favour with God and man."

God will give us wisdom if we ask for it.

Ephesians 1:17 says, "That the God of our Lord Jesus Christ, the Father of glory, may give unto you the spirit of wisdom and revelation in the knowledge of him."

Not only will God give His prophets wisdom but revelation to know Him better. This is why prophets are faithful because they are in constant relationship with Him. Prophets know that God is the ultimate source of wisdom. If they continue to press in to His presence, then the discoveries are endless.

Colossians 2:3 says, "In whom are hid all the treasures of wisdom and knowledge."

God gives wisdom to His people to be skilled in certain areas. Moses had to give instructions from the Lord to skilled craftsmen to whom God had given wisdom (Exodus 35:31, Exodus 36:1).

Exodus 28:2 says, "And thou shalt speak unto all that are wise hearted, whom I have filled with the spirit of wisdom, that they may make Aaron's garments to consecrate him, that he may minister unto me in the priest's office."

Moses was already wise because the Egyptians taught him many things, but God's wisdom took him to another level (Acts 7:22). Since Moses was filled with the Spirit of wisdom, he was able to impart it to his predecessor, Joshua.

Deuteronomy 34:9 says, "And Joshua the son of Nun was full of the spirit of wisdom; for Moses had laid his hands upon him: and the children of Israel hearkened unto him and did as the Lord commanded Moses."

Since Joshua received impartation, he was effectively able to lead the Israelites into the Promised Land. Remember, you can't impart what you don't have. Whatever anointing you have on your life, then you are able to impart it into others. As long as prophets seek God's counsel and get filled with His wisdom, they will not be led astray.

1. How important is wisdom in the prophetic ministry?

2. What are some blessings of being wise?

3. What are some consequences of having a lack of wisdom?

'X'

Prophets are very xenacious. This means that they are filled with yearning for change. This word is obsolete, but its meaning is still relevant. Prophets get bored with the same traditional church service. They love when God does a new thing.

Isaiah 43:18-19 says, "Remember ye not the former things, neither consider the things of old. Behold, I will do a new thing; now it shall spring forth; shall ye not know it? I will even make a way in the wilderness, and rivers in the desert."

They recognize when something is outdated and want to be partakers of the next major move of God.

They want all churches to be filled with the Glory of God and they are able to discern when His Glory isn't present. They want a move of God and they are grieved when each service becomes predictable. They are bothered by a dull service or where the atmosphere is just dry and lacking Glory (1 Samuel 4:21).

Prophets love to worship and love to worship spontaneously as the Spirit of God releases a new sound. Prophets are looking forward to the next move of God.

Philippians 3:13 says, "Brethren, I count not myself to have apprehended: but this one thing I do, forgetting those things which are behind, and reaching forth unto those things which are before."

Prophets are able to tap into the spirit realm and get God's blueprint in order to get a glimpse of what He is about to do in the earth.

Prophets desire to grow spiritually and love the presence of the Lord. They want to grow in God and get more knowledge of Him.

Habakkuk 2:14 says, "For the earth shall be filled with the knowledge of the glory of the Lord, as the waters cover the sea."

Prophets desire for God to bring changes in the nations and for everyone to be able to fellowship with the Holy Spirit. God places the desire for change in His prophets. Don't allow someone to label you as weird or a troublemaker. You are just prophetic and serious about fulfilling your call.

1. What ways do prophets yearn for change?

_____
_____
_____
_____
_____

2. What are some benefits of having prophets involved in the prayer and worship ministry?

3. Why do prophets want others to prophesy and to grow in their spiritual gifts?

'Y'

Yield is another word for submission. Prophets must be yielding to the Spirit of God in order to be effective in their ministry.

1 Peter 5:6 says, "Humble yourselves therefore under the mighty hand of God, that he may exalt you in due time."

Prophets have to yield to the timing of God. They may want to step out and do things on their own, but they have to realize that God's timing is best. When a prophet humbles themselves and trusts the timing of God, then they will be in the perfect alignment. Things will begin to line up and their prophetic agenda will be fulfilled at the right timing. Prophets won't have to stress or worry but God will elevate them and open up the right doors at the right time.

Psalm 40:8 says, "I delight to do thy will, O my God: yea, thy law is within my heart."

Prophets must yield to God's will over their own will because God has the best plan. For instance, they might want to marry a certain person or go certain places. If God says no, then they will have to accept it and obey His voice. Doing God's will shouldn't be grievous or burdensome but a pleasure to do if the prophet keeps their heart pure before the Lord.

James 4:7 says, "Submit yourselves therefore to God. Resist the devil, and he will flee from you."

Prophets will have to submit to God in order to have strength over the enemy. Prophets face many hardships such as persecution and warfare. When they yield to the Spirit of God, they will become lost in their purpose and the attacks of the enemy will not get them off course. They will recognize the bigger purpose behind the demonic opposition, which is the Lord's plan. The enemy will realize that he can't stop God's plan and will flee.

Jesus is the ultimate example of being yielded to God's will.

Luke 22:42 reveals where Jesus was tempted to reject God's plan, yet He yielded, saying, "Father, if thou be willing, remove this cup from me: nevertheless not my will, but thine, be done."

Jesus knew what He had to do and what was required of Him. He spent many hours in prayer before His crucifixion and prayed the prayer in Luke 22:42. Jesus paid the ultimate price in order to do the will of God. No matter what the outcome is, prophets must be willing to pay the price and face consequences, so God can get glorified.

John 12:49-50 says, "For I have not spoken of myself; but the Father which sent me, he gave me a commandment, what I should say, and what I should speak. And I know that his commandment is life everlasting: whatsoever I speak therefore, even as the Father said unto me, so I speak."

Prophets must yield to God in the correct timing of when to release a word. They must yield to the flow of the Holy Spirit and go in the direction He is leading them. For instance, they might want to prophesy but God may want them to operate in healing or deliverance when they are ministering. So, they have to yield to God's Spirit. Also, they have to speak what God tells them to speak and not worry about pleasing men. They have to be careful not to release words that tickle ears but release the true word of God. Prophets must speak what God tells them, even if it has adverse results.

Psalm 119:133 says, "Order my steps in thy word: and let not any iniquity have dominion over me."

Prophets have to yield to God's word and crucify their fleshy desires. Sin must not take reign in a prophet's heart. Prophets must pray to have God order their steps in His word and for God to guide their footsteps. As you yield to the plans and purposes of God, your life and ministry will be fruitful, productive, and blessed.

1. Define the term yield.

   _____
   _____
   _____
   _____
   _____

2. Why must prophets be yielded to God?

   _____
   _____
   _____
   _____
   _____

3. What are some consequences of having a lack of submission to God?

_____
_____
_____
_____
_____

'Z'

Prophets have great zeal or enthusiasm about their calling. They may not feel like this at first but eventually they will. They are ministers of fire (Hebrews 1:7). Elijah was very zealous over the Lord. He served Him faithfully despite the difficulty he faced. Prophets of today have to do the same. Where's your zeal? Where's your fight? Have you lost your fire? Have you lost your passion about the things of God?

1 Kings 19:9-10 says, "And he came thither unto a cave, and lodged there; and, behold, the word of the Lord came to him, and he said unto him, What doest thou here, Elijah? And he said, I have been very jealous for the Lord God of hosts: for the children of Israel have forsaken thy covenant, thrown down thine altars, and slain thy prophets with the sword; and I, even I only, am left; and they seek my life, to take it away."

Prophets must never lose their zeal when God corrects them. They must realize that God chastises them because He loves them.

Revelation 3:19 says, "As many as I love, I rebuke and chasten: be zealous therefore, and repent."

Prophets must have a repenting heart and keep the right attitude in their ministry. They can't be lazy but be consistent.

Romans 12:11 says, "Not slothful in business [zeal]; fervent in spirit; serving the Lord" (Emphasis mine).

Titus 2:14 says, "Who gave himself for us, that he might redeem us from all iniquity, and purify unto himself a peculiar people, zealous of good works."

God has set His prophets apart and expects them to be full of righteous zeal and to do great works that bring Him glory. Jesus came to set the captive free by redeeming us from all iniquity. Prophets have a burning desire for everyone to know God. They desire that people get saved regardless if they are considered their enemy.

Psalm 119:139 says, "My zeal hath consumed me, because mine enemies have forgotten thy words."

Prophets must keep the passion of God strong in their lives and they will be world changers.

1. Define the term zealous.

_____
_____
_____
_____
_____

2. What are the dangers of losing zeal for the things of God?

_____

_____

_____

_____

_____

3. How can someone keep their zeal strong for God?

_____

_____

_____

_____

About The Author

Kimberly Moses started off her ministry as Kimberly Hargraves. She is highly sought after as a prophetic voice, intercessor and prolific author. There is no doubt that she has a global mandate on her life to serve the nations of the world by spreading the Gospel of Jesus Christ. She has a quickly expanding worldwide healing and deliverance ministry. Kimberly Moses wears many hats to fulfill the call God has placed on her life as an entrepreneur over several businesses including her own personal brand Rejoice Essentials which promotes the Gospel of Jesus Christ.

She also serves as a life coach and mentor to many women. She is also the loving mother of two wonderful children. She is married to Tron. Kimberly has dedicated her life to the work of ministry and to serve others under the call God has placed over her life. Kimberly currently resides in South Carolina.

She is a very anointed woman of God who signs, miracles and wonders follow. The miraculous and incessant testimonies attributed to her ministry are incalculable, with many reporting physical and mental healing, financial breakthroughs, debt cancellations and other favorable outcomes. She is known across the globe as a servant who truly labors on behalf of God's people through intercession.

She is the author of The Following:

"Overcoming Difficult Life Experiences with Scriptures and Prayers"
"Overcoming Emotions with Prayers"
"Daily Prayers That Bring Changes"
"In Right Standing,"
"Obedience Is Key,"
"Prayers That Break The Yoke Of The Enemy: A Book Of Declarations,"
"Prayers That Demolish Demonic Strongholds: A Book Of Declarations,"
"Work Smarter. Not Harder. A Book Of Declarations For The Workforce,"
"Set The Captives Free: A Book Of Deliverance."
"Pray More Challenge"

"Walk By Faith: A Daily Devotional"
"Empowering The New Me: Fifty Tips To Becoming A Godly Woman"
"School of the Prophets: A Curriculum For Success"
"8 Keys To Accessing The Supernatural"
"Conquering The Mind: A Daily Devotional"
"Enhancing The Prophetic In You"

You can find more about Kimberly at www.kimberlyhargraves.com

References

1. Anointing. NAS Exhaustive Concordance of the Bible with Hebrew-Aramaic and Greek Dictionaries. Copyright © 1981, 1998 by The Lockman Foundation All rights reserved Lockman.org
2. "Just." Merriam-Webster.com. Merriam-Webster, n.d. Web. 11 Mar. 2018.
3. "Woe." Merriam-Webster.com. Merriam-Webster, n.d. Web. 12 Mar. 2018.
4. "Noble." Merriam-Webster.com. Merriam-Webster, n.d. Web. 6 May 2018.
5. "Quaint." Merriam-Webster.com. Merriam-Webster, n.d. Web. 10 May 2018.
6. "Tranquil." Merriam-Webster.com. Merriam-Webster, n.d. Web. 10 May 2018.
7. "Valiant." Merriam-Webster.com. Merriam-Webster, n.d. Web. 17 May 2018.

Index

A

anointing, 5–6, 8–9, 11, 119, 140
assignment, 5–6, 10, 33, 85, 116, 120, 124, 130, 135
atonement, 58, 104
attacks, 16, 35, 47, 53, 66, 68, 125–26, 134, 148

B

battles, 15, 29, 134, 136
blessings, 9, 26, 38, 81, 96, 141
boldness, 12, 14–15

C

captive, 41, 154
carnal mind, 82
casting, 8, 14
character, 2–3, 95, 106

commandments, 109, 111, 149
confirmation, 25
correction, 18–23
crowd, 108, 111–12
crucifixion, 148

D

dangers, 82, 88, 117, 122, 155
deliveance, 32–33, 36, 70, 149
demons, 14
destruction, 62, 68
directives, 24–25, 28, 30
disciples, 21, 29, 120
disobedience, 99, 101
disturbance, 123

E

emotions, 32, 34, 37–39, 54, 129
enemies, 14–16, 21, 29, 35, 43, 47, 53–54, 68, 75, 80, 125–26, 130–31, 133–34, 148, 154

F

forgiveness, 43–45, 49–50, 67

G

generations, 67–68
glory, 4, 62, 67, 143–44, 154
gospel, 75
grace, 53

H

healing, 8, 14, 129, 149
hearts, 13, 20, 33, 37, 43, 52–53, 73–74, 77, 79, 89–90, 95, 99–100, 114–15, 131, 147
Holy Ghost, 29
Hosea, 98, 103
humility, 62–65

I

instructions, 26, 28–29, 39, 84, 116, 139
intercession, 63, 67
intercessors, 66, 70–71

J

Jahaziel, 28

Jesus, 4, 8, 13–15, 21, 40, 44–45, 58, 61, 67, 79, 86, 128, 138, 148, 154
Jonah, 33–34
judgment, 33, 37, 74–75

K

kingdom, 78–81, 124
Kingdom of God, 15, 59, 79, 81, 111
knowledge, 79, 125, 138–39, 144

L

leaders, 14, 115
longsuffering, 19, 83, 88
love, 33, 43, 46, 48, 55, 67, 73, 131, 142–44
Luke, 21, 29, 44, 86, 131, 138, 148

M

meditation, 90–92
mercy, 44, 48
Messiah, 102–4
minds, 40, 45, 77, 87, 90, 95, 120, 123–24, 126
miracles, 13, 52, 64

miracle worker, 53

N

noble, 93, 96, 156

P

passion, 152, 154
patient, 19, 83, 86
peace, 40, 124, 135, 138
persecution, 127–28, 148
power, 8, 14, 35, 55–57, 59, 81
pray, 3–4, 43, 48, 67, 114, 116, 131, 150
prayer, 3, 32, 34, 36, 41, 67–68, 114, 123, 134, 145, 148
pride, 62
promises, 28, 68, 83
prophets, 8, 13, 18, 33, 36, 45, 75, 81–82, 84, 109, 115, 120, 124
prophecies, 6, 24–27, 29–30, 44, 75, 89, 102
prophesy, 16, 91, 102, 145, 149

Q

quaint, 106–10

R

rebukes, 19, 21–22
redemption, 46
rejoice, 48, 53
remission, 44–45
repentance, 20, 74, 76
revelation, 139
righteousness, 16, 20, 57, 77, 138
rock, 39–40, 53

S

sacrifices, 27, 79, 103, 111, 118–20, 122
Sacrificial, 118
sight, 15, 37, 39, 43
sins, 37, 44–46, 58, 74, 76, 96, 115
spiritual eyes, 53
submission, 146, 151
supernatural, 40
supplication, 123

T

tranquility, 126

trials, 2, 95, 97
trust, 52–53

U

unforgiveness, 46, 49

V
valiant, 133–34, 136

victory, 29, 55
voice, 73, 104–5, 108, 115, 125, 147

W

water, 28, 39
wealth, 56
wisdom, 2, 57, 137–39, 141
worship, 143

Z

zeal, 152–53, 155
zealous, 152, 154

www.ingramcontent.com/pod-product-compliance
Lightning Source LLC
Chambersburg PA
CBHW052132110526
44591CB00012B/1684